Wildflowers
of the
White Mountains

Wildflowers
of the
White Mountains

*An Introduction to
Wildflowers Commonly Found in
New Hampshire's White Mountains*

John Hession
Valerie Michaud

HUNTINGTON
GRAPHICS

First Edition 2003
First Printing
© 2003 Huntington Graphics, all rights reserved
Printed in Canada

Publisher: Huntington Graphics
          P. O. Box 373
          Burlington, VT 05402

Book design: Andrea Gray
Cover design: Lars Gange and JP McGarrity —
          Black Bullet.com

Includes index.
ISBN 1-886064-16-4

Photo Credits — All photos were taken by the authors except as noted:
Sarah T. Schwaegler photographed the Round-lobed Hepatica, p.12,
Closed Gentian, p. 19, Marsh Skullcap, p. 30, Mad Dog Skullcap, p.
31, Small Purple-fringed Orchid, p. 36, Marsh Blue Violet, p. 47,
Nodding Burr Marigold, p. 56, Tall Coneflower, p. 64, White Wood
Aster, p. 113, Nodding Ladies Tresses, p. 160, Yellow Nodding Ladies Tresses, p. 161, Mountain Sandwort, p. 167, Pitcher Plant, p.
227, Northern Green Orchid, p. 253, and Round-leaved Orchid, p.
255. John R. Williams photographed the Round-leaved Ragwort,
p. 61, Hooded Ladies Tresses, p. 162, Rose Pogonia, p. 220, Spotted
Coral Root, p. 250, and Club Spur Orchis, p. 252. John Williams
photographs copyright 2001-2 USDA, used by permission. Blue Eyed
Grass, p. 23, was taken by James F. Fitz. The authors' photographs
were taken using Nikkor lenses on Nikon D-1 and D-1H professional digital cameras and Nikon FM-2 and F5 35mm cameras.

Acknowledgements

We would like to thank the people who have generously helped in the creation of this book. We thank Dorothy Zug for her encouragement of this project in its initial stages. We have deep gratitude for the insightful guidance and direction provided to us by Amey Bailey. In addition, we would like to thank Lionel Chute of New Hampshire Natural Heritage for his comments and helpful suggestions. We also thank David and Tanya Tellman for their kind assistance with our photography. We especially thank Sarah T. Schwaegler for her valuable refinement of our list of species and for providing us with beautiful photographs to help complete our image collection. In addition, we are deeply indebted to John R. Williams, who generously shared his in-depth knowledge of these mountains and has been an invaluable resource in helping us focus our efforts and bring depth and variety to this guide. John William's photographs, like Sarah's, have enriched the scope of this book.

We also extend sincere thanks to all the people who have contributed to this effort including our friends, our publisher, our designer, members and staff of the New Hampshire Audubon Society, the Society for the Protection of New Hampshire Forests, the New Hampshire Natural Heritage Bureau at the New Hampshire Department of Resources and Economic Development's Division of Forests and Lands, the U. S. Forest Service, the staff at Hubbard Brook Experimental Forest, the Weeks State Park Association, and the naturalists on staff at the Appalachian Mountain Club's huts and lodges. We also thank Jay Buckley, of Megaprint in Holderness, New Hampshire for the generous donation of film scanning. In addition, the authors would like to thank the technical support and service staff at Nikon USA. Their commitment to the professional photographer and their unparalleled and timely support proved invaluable. We also thank Bill Nichols of New Hampshire Natural Heritage who professionally reviewed our final manuscript.

Finally, the authors would like to dedicate this book to their families whose love and encouragement made this book possible.

About the Authors: John Hession and Valerie Michaud are amateur naturalists who live in central New Hampshire at the southern edge of the White Mountain National Forest. They met as rock climbing partners and this book is an outgrowth of their joint efforts photographing wildflowers while climbing and exploring the White Mountains. John works as a free lance commercial photographer in Plymouth, New Hampshire. Valerie works at Dartmouth Hitchcock Medical Center in the Radiology Department.

Contents

Authors' Foreword

Wildflowers paint the White Mountains with splashes of color in spring, summer and fall, awakening the senses and inspiring all who view them. Wildflowers are treasures to behold, a wonderful gift to all who visit these mountains.

View of Mt. Washington

How many times have you looked out over a field, or along the side of a country road, or at some corner of the forest and asked yourself: What flower is that?

We decided to answer that question with a pocket field guide that would inspire and inform.

As we climbed these mountains and walked through surrounding fields and wetlands we photographed each new flower we encountered. You are likely to encounter these same flowers as you explore the White Mountains and their foothills.

These flowers are wonderfully intricate. They exhibit fine structures and beautiful details. We have photographed the flowers to depict the features that make each flower unique. We captured images of these flowers in their natural setting so that they will appear as you see them in the wild.

Some wildflowers are small and easily overlooked. In such cases we have photographed using a close-up lens that brings the small blossoms into sharp focus. Many wildflower enthusiasts find that a small magnifying glass or inexpensive photo

Canada Mayflower

Grass Pink, a native Orchid

loupe is a great addition to their backpack.

Large Purple-fringed Orchid

Many of the wildflowers in this book have interesting histories and origins. Some were used by Native American tribes for food, medicine and ritual. Others were introduced by European colonists who brought many species with them as they crossed the Atlantic to North America.

Some wildflowers are not what they seem: flowers in the aster family are actually clusters of many small flowers tightly bunched together.

Kidney-leaf Buttercup

Lilacs, seen here near Mt. Chocorua, were introduced to New Hampshire by colonial governor Benning Wentworth in 1750.

A single Daisy flower head is actually composed of hundreds of small tube and ray shaped flowers.

Butterfly and Milkweed

Wildflowers are an important food source for insects, wild birds, and other animals, which in turn help pollinate the flowers they feed on.

As you use this guide to explore the wildflowers of the White Mountains we hope you will reflect on the valuable resource these flowers represent. There are many fine membership organizations dedicated to education, stewardship, conservation and development of our wilderness resources. Consult *Wildflower Resources* on page 275 for more information on these organizations.

The over 250 flowers illustrated in these pages are prominent representatives of over 3500 species of flowers that grow wild in New England. They are a window into the vast diversity of life which comprises our world and which supports our existence. The flowers found in just this small corner of New England represent only a small fraction of the rich fabric of plant life which is the foundation of all other life on this planet.

Many wildflowers have declining populations due to over-picking, development and displacement by invasive species. Within the White Mountain National Forest, picking wildflowers is prohibited without a re-

Wildflowers provide valuable food for wildlife.

search permit. In addition, threatened and endangered wildflowers are protected by state law throughout New Hampshire.

If you wish to share your wildflower discoveries, photographs are a wonderful way to document your sightings. Please share what you have found with others by leaving the wildflowers untouched in their natural environment.

Introduction

■ **Geographic range:** This book covers wildflowers commonly found in the White Mountain National Forest, in nearby State Parks, and on other public lands in the surrounding foothills. We have also included the Appalachian Trail Corridor in New Hampshire.

■ **Flower species included in this guide:** We have included most of the common wildflowers we encoun-

Cannon Cliff in Franconia Notch State Park

tered while hiking and climbing in this area. Our choice of flowers has been influenced by consultation with naturalists, scientists and amateur botanists whose collective experience has refined our list of species to include prominent and common representatives of most wildflower families found in the White Mountains.

We have included many common roadside flowers as well as deep woodland and wetland plants found in more remote regions. This guide also covers many of the alpine flowers that a hiker is likely to encounter above treeline at higher elevations. We have also included a few favorite flowering woody plants such as Crab Apple, and Lilac, the New Hampshire state flower.

However, in a pocket guide it is difficult to show all the flowers a visitor might encounter. Some wildflower families, such as the Asters, have hundreds of species growing in the White Mountains. For example, over 25 species of Goldenrod, all members of the Aster family, grow in the White Mountains. This guide contains the Canadian Goldenrod, The Lance-leaved Goldenrod, The Rough-stemmed Goldenrod and the Silverrod. We have chosen these species to illustrate the range and beauty of flowers in this plant group.

If you find a flower that is not listed in our guide you can often identify it by using one of the many fine botanical references listed in *Further Reading* on page 269.

First, find the flower in our book that is most similar in appearance to the flower you are trying to identify. Chances are that they are closely related and may share the same family and genus name. Make a note of any physical differences between the two flowers.

Then consult one of the botanical references. These reference guides have comprehensive keys that distinguish closely related species based upon physical characteristics, such as leaf shape, stem hairs, flower structure, etc. Many of these are available through local and university libraries.

■ **What are wildflowers?** Wildflowers are generally defined as flowering plants which grow and reproduce successfully on their own without cultivation. Naturalists distinguish two main categories of wild flowers, *native* and *naturalized.*

A colony of Yellow Lady's Slipper

■ **Native Flowers:** Native flowering plants are those which were not introduced to the region by human activity. Native flowers generally migrated to the White Mountains as the glaciers which covered New Hampshire receded northward at the end of the last Ice Age approximately 14,000 years ago. Native flowering plants, and many non-natives as well, are well adapted to the harsh conditions that prevail in the White Mountains, and are found in both disturbed and undisturbed natural settings, such as deep forests, marshes, riverbanks, bogs and mountain sides.

■ **Naturalized Flowers:** In the recent past, human activity has introduced many new species to the White Mountains. Over time many of these plants found a place in local plant communities, and thus became naturalized: *they reproduce successfully outside of cultivation.* These species often flourish near developed, disturbed areas and are often seen along roads, in fields and on recently cleared lands with some of our native flora.

For example, it is believed that as Native American tribes moved into this region after the last ice age they brought with them flowering plants used as medicines, to dye clothing and to create artwork.

Later, European settlers brought many types of plants with them, for food, as medicines and as ornamental plants. Colonists often considered the seeds they brought with them to be one of their most valuable possessions. An examination of the foundations of abandoned farm houses and out-buildings reveals many of these species. Other naturalized plants were brought here by European settlers accidentally, as "stowaways."

More recently, wildflower gardening movements have introduced new wildflowers from all around the world to the White Mountains. Some escaped cultivation and where they found suitable local conditions, became naturalized in the landscape.

In addition, the vast transportation infrastructure has facilitated the spread of many naturalized species. Seeds and plants are picked up and transported, sometimes inadvertently, into this region.

Rainbow over Pinkam Notch.

■ **Invasive Plants:** Some of these naturalized species, such as Yellow Flag Iris, are invasive and can disrupt native plant communities. In fact, a significant threat to native plants in some areas in the White Mountains is the loss of habitat due to invasions by aggressive non-native species. Some invasive species initially arrive as garden plants which then escape cultivation and establish themselves in the wild. Purple Loosestrife is a good example. Although its deep purple blooms are admired by many, it often takes over adjoining wetlands, eventually replacing nearly all other native species which existed before its escape. As a result, some species such as Purple Loosestrife are now illegal to cultivate in New Hampshire. It is considered unwise to introduce potentially invasive species into new areas.

How to Use this Guide

■ **Organization of the Flower Pages:** To facilitate identification we have grouped the wildflowers in this guide by their main color:

- Blue to Purple
- Orange
- Yellow
- White
- Pink to Red
- Green to Brown

Within each color section, the plants are organized alphabetically by their family name. This places flowers with similar characteristics near each other. Flowers within each family are then listed alphabetically by their genus and species name.

Many flowers have variations in their color. Please check other color sections if you cannot find the flower you are looking for. For example, many light pink or blue flowers have white variations.

A white variety of the Pink Lady's Slipper

■ **Photographs:** Each flower has been photographed to illustrate the natural beauty and structure of the flower as seen in the wild. The flower size noted at the bottom of the page will give you an idea of the photograph's magnification or reduction.

■ **Common Name:** Wildflowers often have many common names. For example Pink Lady's Slipper is also known as Moccasin Flower and Nerve-root. We have used the common name that is generally in use in New England.

■ **Scientific Name:** For most genus and species names we follow the evolving Flora of North America online database at www.FNA.org/FNA/. Please note that some of the species covered in this book have recently been given new scientific names as a result of current research and genetic surveys. Our index includes both the current and former scientific names of plants that have been recently reclassified. For example if you look up *Hepatica americana*, which is the former scientific name for Round-lobed Hepatica, our index will direct you to the current scientific name, which is *Anemone americana*.

■ **Description:** We start with the common family name. We generally follow Flora of the Northeast (Magee and Ahles, 2000). We use the common family names rather than the scientific family names (i.e., Mint vs. Lamiaceae) because the scientific family names are not generally well known.

We then describe the important features of the flower head, flower arrangement, leaves and features distinctive to the flower. We also discuss the general setting in which the plant can be found, and whether it is considered to be native or naturalized. Finally, we note interesting historical or medicinal uses.

In describing plant structures we have used non-technical terms whenever appropriate. However, describing flowers without using terms such as petal, sepal, stamen and pistil is like trying to describe the human body without using words such as leg, arm, head or torso. We have included a *Glossary* of botanical terms to explain

Leaf of the carnivorous Pitcher Plant

terms used in this guide. We also have included an *Illustrated Glossary* which contains illustrations that depict the structures of flowers, leaves, stems and stalks. Please give our glossaries a quick read and consult them as needed.

■ **Size:** Size refers to the dimension of the head of the flower. If we refer to the size of a cluster of flower heads, or part of a flower head it is so noted after the size.

■ **Height:** Height refers to the overall height of the plant above the ground. Sometimes the flower head (as in Wild Ginger and Skunk Cabbage) is much lower than the top of the plant or grows on the ground.

■ **Blooms:** Blooms refers to a general range of flowering time. Actual bloom time in any location is variable. In more northern and higher elevation areas, bloom times are generally later. In addition, local factors such as prevailing weather and the amount of leaf canopy over the flower can alter the time of bloom from year to year.

Bluet with five petals

Finally, many flowers vary in shape, size and color from specimen to specimen depending on growing conditions and time of year. A common blue violet can have half-inch flowers in a poor growing season and one-inch flowers the following year. A spring frost can fade a Wild Columbine's vibrant red petals to a light pink. Some species, like the Bluet, have variation in the number of petals from flower to flower. Use our descriptions and dimensions as a starting point.

White Mountain Overview

■ **The White Mountain Environment:** Most White Mountain wildflowers moved into the region gradually over the last 14,000 years. Prior to that time all of New Hampshire was covered by an ice sheet up to a mile thick. As the ice melted and retreated north it left behind impressive notches, valleys, and huge piles of rock and boulders. Flowers and other plants moved north and populated the area though the natural evolution and succession of plant communities. This process was influenced by changes in temperature, rainfall, and the development of soils as glaciers retreated and the climate gradually warmed. In addition, animal migration affected the distribution of plants that depend on animals for seed dispersal and pollination. Over several thousand years this process established the upland and wetland communities that form the home of many flowers in this guide.

The White Mountains were almost completely logged during the late 19th century. Concern over the loss of old growth forests and diminishing opportunities for wilderness conservation and recreation led eventually to the establishment of the White Mountain National Forest. Continuing efforts by conservation and preservation groups have helped protect additional upland and wetland habitat.

Despite the widespread deforestation of this region over a century ago most of the White Mountains are again covered with forest. This forest is part of a much larger ecosystem called the Great North Woods, which extends from southern Canada through northeastern

Cotton Sedge in an alpine bog on Mt. Madison

Sphagnum moss bog

United States and west as far as the Great Lakes Region. This forest is characterized by long cold winters, a short growing season and high levels of precipitation.

■ **Natural Communities:** Natural communities are recurring assemblages of plants and animals found in particular physical settings. Over 200 natural communities occur in New Hampshire from high salt marshes to alpine meadows, rich mesic forests to dry river bluffs. The White Mountains, because of their diverse elevation and extensive range of soil conditions, contain most of the natural communities found in the North Woods, including sphagnum moss bogs and alpine communities. As you hike or drive through the mountains you can see the different natural communities next to each other. In one place you can be overlooking a lakeside marsh, then just a few hundred yards away, you may cross into a mixed hardwood and spruce forest. The plants and flowers found in neighboring natural communities may often be quite different.

The type of natural community which is found in a given area of the White Mountains depends on environmental factors such as soil composition, underlying rocks and minerals, rainfall, soil moisture, temperature, the amount of sunlight and human impacts.

Colony of native violets

Most wildflowers can be found in several different natural communities. For example, Bunchberry can be found in lowland spruce forest communities. Bunchberry can also be found in sub-alpine communities near the summits of the Presidential Range. Another plant, Goldthread, is found in both low elevation swamps and alpine wetlands.

Bunchberry in pine forest

The natural communities found in the White Mountains are grouped into six basic ecological settings.

■ **Forests:** Forests are generally defined as having over 60% tree cover. These include spruce-fir forests, beech-birch-maple forests and oak-pine forests. The flowers found in these forests depend upon the underlying soil conditions. Some species, such as Dutchman's Breeches, Squirrel Corn, Hepatica and Ginseng are found only in soils rich in calcium. Other plants, such as Clintonia, Pink Lady's Slipper, Canada Mayflower, Wood Sorrel and Sarsaparilla are much less discriminating and can be found in a variety of forest communities.

■ **Woodlands:** Woodland areas support 25% to 60% tree cover. These are areas where natural conditions, (such as weather, periodic fires, floods, lack of soil, wet soils, the steepness of mountain slopes, or high elevation) limit the

Fringed Polygala in woodland setting

growth of tree cover. Plants such as Rhodora and Herb Robert can be found in woodland communities.

■ **Meadows and Barrens:** Here the tree cover is less than 25% or even nonexistent. These areas include sub-alpine rocky summits, exposed cliff sides, talus slopes, river banks and the highest reaches of the White Mountains, the alpine zone. Diverse types of wildflowers are found in these open communities, including Bunchberry, Canada Mayflower, Goldthread, Wild

Alpine community near Tuckerman Ravine

Columbine and Harebell. In higher elevation communities Three-Toothed Cinquefoil, Diapensia, Alpine Bilberry and Mountain Avens are seen.

■ **Forested Wetlands:** Forested wetlands include natural communities such as swamps, floodplain forests, and temporarily flooded basins known as vernal pools. Trees can include Red Maple, Silver Maple, Ash and Cedar. Wildflowers found in these communities include Touch-me-not, Tall Meadow-rue, Swamp Candles, Marsh Marigold, False Hellebore and Blue Flag Iris.

■ **Open Wetlands:** Open wetlands include streamside and lakeside marshes, peat bogs, (also known as fens) and seeps (where ground water seeps to the surface, usually carrying dissolved nutrients needed for plant growth). Bog Laurel, Foam Flower, Pitcher Plant, Blue Marsh Violet and the Purple-stemmed Aster can be found in these communities.

Pickerelweed in a swamp community

■ **Ponds, Lakes and Rivers:** Ponds, lakes and rivers are found throughout the mountains, and can vary from small alpine ponds to large bodies of water. Water Lilies, Monkey Flower, St. John's Wort, and Arrowhead are often found in these communities.

Lakeside marsh

Lost Pond near Mt. Washington

As you look for wildflowers it is helpful to identify the setting in which they grow. Many wildflowers are easy to spot once you have identified the natural community in the area you are exploring.

■ **A Note on Species at Risk.** As you read through this book you will notice that some species are considered uncommon or rare. In addition, several species depicted in this book are noted as threatened, endangered or on watch. If you think you have seen one of these species in the wild, please do not disturb the plant. Make careful notes of the location and contact the New Hampshire Natural Heritage Bureau. NHNHB is the the state program, run under the Division of Forests and Lands, that finds, tracks and facilitates the protection of New Hampshire's rare plants. For contact information and a discussion of efforts to protect rare species, please see *Species at Risk* on page 273.

■ **A Note on Biodiversity.** Wildflowers found in natural communities contribute to interdependent groups of plant and animal life. Flowering plants play an important role in the food chain of insects and and other animals. Their continued presence is necessary to sustain wildlife.

Many wildflowers are scarce and easily harmed. In addition, due to widespread deforestation during the last century, some of the natural communities found in the area's forests, parks and nature preserves are the last mature surviving examples of these communities in the region.

Although it may not be possible to precisely value the contribution of any one particular plant or animal species, scientists generally agree that maintaining biodiversity is the best way to insure a healthy environment and minimize the negative impacts of certain disturbances.

Moose enjoying his breakfast

The flowers depicted in these pages are a small but important part of the extraordinary biodiversity that underlies our natural world and makes our forests, parks and nature preserves a valuable resource for us all.

■ **A Note on Medicinal and Edible Plants.** Many flowering plants listed in this book were historically eaten or used for medicine. However, using wild plants for food or medicine is best left to experts. Some plants are edible only in a certain season, or require special preparation to eliminate toxins. In addition, some plants have lookalikes that are not edible. Many historical medicinal uses of wild plants are now known to be ineffective or dangerous. The listings this book of historical food and medicinal uses of flowering plants are for reference only.

Brown Knapweed   *Centaurea jacea*

ASTER FAMILY. Flower heads, composed of many rose-purple disk flowers, are supported by a base of scaly brown-toothed overlapping bracts. One to many flower heads appear singly on branches and terminal stems of this naturalized European aster. Narrow, unstalked, upper leaves and stalked, lobed or toothed, lower leaves alternate up the stem. Forms colorful colonies in fields and along roads where it attracts many bees and butterflies for pollination. The American Goldfinch frequently feeds on this plant's seeds.

FLOWER: 1¾"   **HEIGHT:** 1'–3'   **BLOOMS:** June–Sept.

Chickory   *Cichorium intybus*

ASTER FAMILY. Vivid blue flowers composed entirely
of rays with square, finely notched tips, and blue anthers in the flower center, distinguish this relative of
the Dandelion. Its nearly leafless stalk has dandelion-
like basal leaves. Often used as an additive or substitute
for coffee. Chickory was an important edible herb for
early European settlers because its high vitamin C content could help prevent scurvy. This naturalized European immigrant is found in fields, pastures and open
woodlands.

FLOWER: 1¹/₂"   **HEIGHT:** 1'–3'   **BLOOMS:** June–Oct.

Bull Thistle   *Cirsium vulgare*

ASTER FAMILY. Brilliant purple to red rayless disk flowers sit atop small black-tipped spiny globes on distinctive winged branches with very long, sharp spines. This plant flowers in the second year. In its first year its tuber-like roots can be cooked and eaten. This naturalized Eurasian thistle is considered potentially invasive and can be found in logged areas, open fields and pastures.

FLOWER: 1"–2"   **HEIGHT:** 2'–6'   **BLOOMS:** June–Sept.

3

Pale Purple Coneflower   *Echinacea pallida*

ASTER FAMILY. Large daisy-like flower with light pink-purple rays drooping backwards from a large, spine-covered central disk. Leaves are lance-shaped with smooth edges. This flower and the similar Purple Coneflower are farmed commercially to make a cold remedy from their roots. Although it is not generally considered naturalized in New Hampshire, it is seen in fields and meadows in northeastern areas of the White Mountains.

FLOWER: 1"–2" disk   **HEIGHT:** 2'–3'   **BLOOMS:** June–Aug.

Robin's Plantain   *Erigeron pulchellus*

ASTER FAMILY. Terminal clusters of one to six pale lavender to violet flowers grow on this downy native fleabane. Numerous petal-like rays surround a prominent yellow center of disk flowers. Leaves are alternate, blunt-toothed and grow up a softly haired stem with broader long-stalked leaves at the stem's base. This plant spreads by runners and is found in open woods, in fields, and along the edges of streams.

FLOWER: 1"–1½"   **HEIGHT:** 10"–24"   **BLOOMS:** April–July

Tall Blue Lettuce

Lactuca biennis

ASTER FAMILY. Many Dandelion-like small pale-blue flowers occur in long loose clusters on an upright stem. Variable lettuce-like leaves, deeply lobed to long lance-shaped, toothed and stalkless grow on smooth stems amid and below flowers. If crushed, a milky sap emerges from leaves and branches. Found in moist clearings, thickets, fields and roadside ditches. This native lettuce has a bitter taste and was used in salads and cooked as greens by European settlers.

FLOWER: 1/4"   HEIGHT: 2'–10'   BLOOMS: July-Sept.

New England Aster
Symphyotrichum novae-angliae

ASTER FAMILY. Clusters of purple-rose ray flowers with yellow disk flowers appear on short stalks that branch from stiff hairy stems. Leaves are alternate, entire, lance-shaped and clasp the stem. Distinctive gland-tipped hairs appear on the flower stalks and on small bracts just beneath the flower head. This large native aster is found in moist areas of hillsides, abandoned fields and meadows. Its seeds and leaves are an important food for game birds and mammals.

FLOWER: 1"–2"   **HEIGHT:** 2'–6'   **BLOOMS:** Aug.–Oct.

Purple-stemmed Aster

Symphyotrichum puniceum

ASTER FAMILY. Striking two-toned composite flower heads are composed of many purple rays surrounding a flat central disk of minute yellow flowers. Flower heads, each on their own stalk, appear in clusters above stout hairy, sometimes purple, central stems. Leaves are shallowly toothed, lance-shaped and smooth. This native aster is found in wet areas of woods and meadows, along streams and on riverbanks.

FLOWER: 1"–1 ½"   **HEIGHT:** 2'–6'   **BLOOMS:** Aug.–Oct.

Harebell   *Campanula rotundifolia*

BELLFLOWER FAMILY. Small blue-violet nodding bell-shaped flowers appear on separate stalks that branch from tall thin stems. The blue corolla is divided into five slightly recurved pointed petal-like lobes. The stem has long narrow alternate upper leaves with roundish leaves at the base. This beautiful native flower is found on rocky slopes, in alpine areas and in dry open woods and fields.

FLOWER: 1"   **HEIGHT:** 6"–18"   **BLOOMS:** July-Sept.

9

Indian Tobacco   *Lobelia inflata*

BELLFLOWER FAMILY. Bluish-purple, two-lipped flowers grow singly from the leaf axils or at the end of stems. Flowers have two upper lobes and three lower lobes. This flower's ovary becomes inflated as the flower fruits. Leaves are oval and toothed, with a hairy underside and they alternate on hairy branching stems. This native plant grows in poor soil of fields, meadows, open woods and along roadways. Once smoked by Native Americans, it is no longer smoked because it contains the alkaloid lobeline, a deadly poison.

FLOWER: ¼"   **HEIGHT:** 1'–3'   **BLOOMS:** June–Sept.

True Forget-me-not   *Myosotis scorpioides*

BORAGE FAMILY. Clusters of sky-blue flowers on coiled branches that unfold as the flower blooms. Funnel-shaped flowers have five petal-like lobes around a yellow center. Alternate, oblong, hairy leaves grow upward close to stem. The coiled curves of the flower branches are said to resemble "scorpion's tails" hence, its Latin name. An important nectar flower in its native European surroundings, it is considered potentially invasive in the White Mountains. It is found in wet meadows, marshes and near streams.

FLOWER: ¼"   **HEIGHT:** 6"–24"   **BLOOMS:** May–Oct.

Round-lobed Hepatica *Anemone americana*

Buttercup family. Groups of lavender to white flowers grow near each other on their own hairy leafless stalks. Flowers have five to nine round petal-like sepals, numerous stamens and many pistils. Surrounding each flower are three broad oval bracts. Leaves with three round lobes and hairy leaf stalks grow from the base of the plant. The name "hepatica," Latin for liver, was given because its leaves resemble liver and it was used in ancient times to treat liver disorders. Native to New Hampshire's dry rocky wooded areas.

Flower: 1/2"–1"   **Height:** 4"–6"   **Blooms:** April–May

Periwinkle   *Vinca minor*

DOGBANE FAMILY. A blue-violet flower with five spreading lobes, it has a white star around its center. It grows from short woody stems with lance-shaped, shiny, leather-like leaves that form a dense mat. This naturalized trailing evergreen was introduced from Europe by colonists because it was a soil stabilizer, a garden favorite, and it was used medicinally to settle stomach disorders and to control bleeding. Found in shady wooded areas, near old foundations, and in cemeteries.

FLOWER: 1"   **HEIGHT:** 6"–8"   **BLOOMS:** April–May

13

Fireweed

Epilobium angustifolium

EVENING PRIMROSE FAMILY. Terminal spike-like clusters of showy purple to pink flowers grow in stands creating spires of color. Bees value this native flower for its nectar. Flowers have four round petals, eight stamens and a long whitish style with a cross–shaped stigma. Seedpods are located beneath the flower clusters and release a silky haired seed. This native "Great Willow Herb," an early colonizer of recently burned-off sites, is found in cleared woodlands and at the edges of fields.

FLOWER: 1"   **HEIGHT:** 2'–7'   **BLOOMS:** July–Sept.

Monkey Flower
Mimulus ringens

FIGWORT FAMILY. Blue-purple two-lipped flowers appear on short stalks. The lower lip is three-lobed and has two yellow ridges on its upper side. The lips grow from a five-sided calyx of fused sepals. The square stem has finely toothed, oval, clasping, opposite leaves. This flower's appearance is said to resemble a grinning monkey, hence the common name. This native perennial herb is found near ponds and streams and in wet meadows and marshes.

FLOWER: 1"   **HEIGHT:** 1'–3'   **BLOOMS:** June–Sept.

Blue Toadflax   *Nuttallanthus canadensis*

Figwort family. Many purple-blue flowers alternate
in a terminal cluster. The two-lobed upper lip curls
back revealing two whitish ridges on a lower lip with
three spreading lobes. Thin spurs protrude from the
flower's base. Smooth, shiny, long, narrow leaves alternate on the upper stalk; a rosette of small leaves is
found at the base of the plant. This New Hampshire
native is found in dry sandy fields and on rocky outcrops.

Flower: 1/4"–1/2"   **Height:** 6"–24"   **Blooms:** May–Sept.

American Speedwell *Veronica americana*

FIGWORT FAMILY. One of approximately six native speedwells, this minute corolla flower has four petal-like lobes, each lobe lined with parallel dark blue veins. A prominent pistil emerges from the flower's yellow center. Toothed leaves, getting larger toward the base of the stem, are heart-shaped and either stalkless or short stalked. This native herb is high in vitamin C and Native Americans ate its boiled leaves as greens.

FLOWER: ¼"   **HEIGHT:** 4"–2'   **BLOOMS:** May–July

Common Speedwell   *Veronica officinalis*

FIGWORT FAMILY. Small blue-lavender flowers with four striped lobes and two protruding stamens appear in spike-like terminal clusters. Opposite, oval, finely haired, toothed leaves appear along the length of the plant's creeping stem. This naturalized flower forms deep mats in dry fields and open woods. The common name "speedwell" is thought to come from its use by European settlers to make a quick-acting wound dressing. Other authorities claim the name derives from the "speed" with which its creeping stalks spread.

FLOWER: ¼"   **HEIGHT:** 3"–10"   **BLOOMS:** May–July

Closed Gentian   *Gentiana clausa*

GENTIAN FAMILY. Dark blue-purple, five-lobed corolla flowers grow in dense terminal clusters from the upper leaf axils. Flowers are nearly closed and appear white at their base with white membranes between the lobes. The stem is smooth and unbranched with stalkless lance-shaped leaves growing opposite in whorls beneath the flowers. Native to moist areas of thickets, meadows and woodland borders. Native Americans used the roots of this flower to treat snakebites.

FLOWER: 1"–1½"   **HEIGHT:** 1'–2'   **BLOOMS:** Aug.–Oct.

Wild Geranium   *Geranium maculatum*

GERANIUM FAMILY. Plants with loose clusters of two to five purple-rose colored flowers with five petals, five short pointed sepals, ten stamens and one pistil. Leaves are opposite, deeply toothed, five-lobed and stalked. Longer stalks appear on the basal leaves. This native perennial herb is found in dry to moist soils of woodlands, rocky meadows and shady grassy areas. Native Americans used this plant, crushed, to treat fungal diseases.

FLOWER: 1"–1½"   **HEIGHT:** 1'–2'   **BLOOMS:** May–June

Lapland Rosebay   *Rhododendron lapponicum*

HEATH FAMILY. Purple to magenta corolla flowers have five deeply lobed segments and several protruding stamens. Leather-like leaves are narrowly oval with pointed tips and have scale-like undersides. This rare aromatic, low-growing, native evergreen shrub forms mats above the timberline near protected rocky areas.

FLOWER: 5/8"–1"   **HEIGHT:** 4"–12"   **BLOOMS:** May–July

Blue Flag Iris

Iris versicolor

IRIS FAMILY. Blue-violet flowers have three petals and three petal-like sepals. Wide down-curved petals are streaked with yellow and white veining. This native New Hampshire iris spreads through a creeping rhizome root and sits atop a slender stalk that is taller than its long narrow vertical leaves. Seen in wet meadows, in marshes and along waterways. Handling this plant may cause contact dermatitis.

FLOWER: 2½"–3"   HEIGHT: 2'–3'   BLOOMS: May–June

Blue-eyed Grass   *Sisyrinchium montanum*

IRIS FAMILY. A few small violet-blue flowers with yellow centers sit in a terminal cluster topped by a pointed
bract. This low, slender flower has three petals, three
petal-like sepals and three stamens, all with pointed
tips. Narrow, basal, grass-like leaves vary in length and
grow on twisted stalks. A native New Hampshire
flower, it is found in sunny fields, meadows and on
sandy shores. A favorite food source for wild turkey
and other game birds.

FLOWER: ¹/₂"   HEIGHT: 4–20"   BLOOMS: May–June

Purple Loosestrife   *Lythrum salicaria*

LOOSESTRIFE FAMILY. Tall spikes of numerous magenta flowers in clusters. Each flower has four wrinkled petals and an equal or greater number of stamens. Long, stalkless, lance-shaped leaves grow on the flower stem and heart-shaped leaves appear at the plant's base. Naturalized from Europe, this species is highly invasive and thrives in marshes and wet lowlands where it displaces native species, altering the habitat of waterfowl and other wildlife.

FLOWER: ³/₄"–1¹/₂"   **HEIGHT:** 2'–4'   **BLOOMS:** July–Sept.

Bluets

Houstonia caerulea

MADDER FAMILY. Small delicate funnel-shaped purple-blue flowers with yellow centers and four spreading petal-shaped lobes sit atop thin stalks. Small but visible stamens vary in length. Upper leaves are tiny and opposite on the stem, the basal leaves form a rosette near the ground. Showy dense colonies of this native New Hampshire spring flower are seen in moist grassy areas, on hillsides, in fields and in open woodlands.

FLOWER: ½"   **HEIGHT:** 3"–6"   **BLOOMS:** May–June

Fringed Polygala   *Polygala paucifolia*

Milkwort family. One to three purple-rose colored orchid-like stalked flowers grow from the base of short leafy stems. The three flower petals form a tube with a pink-yellow fringed tip. Five sepals: two are large, lateral and wing-like, the other three are small and obscured. This low-growing native plant has alternate simple oval leaves with pointed tips that emerge from underground stems. It makes evergreen carpets on forest floors in areas with sandy or rich soils.

Flower: 3/4"   **Height:** 3"–6"   **Blooms:** May–June

Bugle-weed

Ajuga reptans

MINT FAMILY. Several bluish-white flowers grow from a leafy terminal spike. Corolla (fused petals) has a short two-lobed upper lip, a three-lobed lower lip, and three protruding stamens. Opposite, stalkless, oblong leaves are blunt-toothed or toothless and grow from a squared, hairy stalk. This perennial herb is naturalized from European gardens and appears near old stone foundations, in fields and in moist areas. Colonists used this plant to treat mouth sores and throat ailments.

FLOWER: ⅛"   **HEIGHT:** 6"–15"   **BLOOMS:** May–June

Gill-over-the-Ground   *Glechoma hederacea*

MINT FAMILY. Small, blue-purple two-lobed flowers with a larger lower lobe. Stamens protrude beneath the upper lobe and tooth-like hairs on the lower lobe give the appearance of a gaping dragon's mouth. Opposite leaves are oval-kidney shaped, short stalked and have shallow rounded teeth. This naturalized European flower spreads quickly by rooting stems. "Gill" is French meaning "to ferment." Prior to the discovery of hops, these flowers were valuable as a fermenting aid in brewing beer. Found in damp woods, in fields and near streams.

FLOWER: ⅓"   **HEIGHT:** 6"–8"   **BLOOMS:** April–July

Heal-all   *Prunella vulgaris*

MINT FAMILY. Flowers form a dense hairy terminal
spike. Flowers are purple-blue, with two-lobed lip petals and four stamens. A broad helmet-shaped upper
lip covers a fringed three-lobed drooping lower lip.
Flower clusters grow above bracts on a squared branching stem. Opposite, lance-shaped, stalked leaves surround the flowers near the stem's base. This naturalized herb is found in pastures, meadows and along
roads. Its name "Heal-All" dates back to the 1700s
when it was used for healing skin wounds.

FLOWER: ½"   **HEIGHT:** 6"–12"   **BLOOMS:** May–Sept.

Marsh Skullcap   *Scutellaria galericulata*

MINT FAMILY. Striking blue and white flowers appear
side by side on short stalks growing on a squared stem
from the base of paired leaves. The flower's upper lip
forms a blue "skullcap" over a whitish, spreading lower
lip. Leaves are arrow-shaped, bluntly toothed, and
stalkless. Medicinal preparations from this native mint,
used in colonial times, are avoided today because they
have been found toxic.

FLOWER: ³/₄"–1"   **HEIGHT:** 2'–3'   **BLOOMS:** July–Aug.

Mad-dog Skullcap — *Scutellaria lateriflora*

MINT FAMILY. Long one-sided clusters of two-lipped blue flowers grow on flower stalks that branch off a square stem near the base of sharply toothed pointed leaves. The upper lip forms a ridged blue cap over the whitish rounded downward-curved lower lip. Formerly used medicinally to treat rabies, hence the common name "Mad-dog" skullcap, it is now considered toxic because it can cause liver damage. This native rhizomatous herb is found in marshes, swamps and wet floodplains.

FLOWER: ½"–⅔"   **HEIGHT:** 1'–2'   **BLOOMS:** July–Aug.

31

Woundwort
Stachys palustris

MINT FAMILY. Pale purple-rose colored flowers appear in whorls of four to eight on an erect hairy square stem. Flowers have a two-lipped corolla: the upper lip is hood-shaped and the lower lip is three-lobed and veined in blue. Leaves are opposite, toothed, lance-shaped and have a hairy upperside. This naturalized European mint is found in wet areas of meadows, woodlands, marshes and roadside ditches.

FLOWER: 1/2"   **HEIGHT:** 8"–2'   **BLOOMS:** June–Sept.

Dame's Rocket · *Hesperis matronalis*

MUSTARD FAMILY. Branched terminal clusters of purple, varying to pink or white, flowers bloom on the tall erect stems of this biennial. Flowers have four wide petals, four hairy sepals and six stamens. Leaves are lance to oval-shaped and toothed. The upper leaves are nearly stalkless and the lower leaves are stalked. This flower's sweet fragrance is more prominent in the evening. Naturalized from Europe, this flower grows near woodland borders, in thickets, and along country roads.

FLOWER: ³/₄"   **HEIGHT:** 1'–4'   **BLOOMS:** April–Aug.

Purple Lilac
Syringa vulgaris

OLIVE FAMILY. Fragrant purple to white flowers appear in terminal clusters at the ends of woody branches with alternate oval leaves. Funnel-shaped flowers have four petal-like lobes spreading backward from the flower's center. Named the New Hampshire State flower because it is a symbol of the hardy character of the "Granite State" people. Lilacs, although generally not considered naturalized, are found where they were previously introduced, near old foundations, in fields, and at abandoned farms.

FLOWER: ½"   HEIGHT: 1'–10'   BLOOMS: June–July

Large Purple-fringed Orchid
Platanthera grandiflora

ORCHID FAMILY. Showy rose-purple and white flowers appear in a vertical spiral on an erect stem. Petals and sepals are the same color: the two upper petals and uppermost sepal form a three-part hood over the large, lacy, fringed lower lip petal. The two lateral sepals form wings off to the side of the lower lip. Large lance-shaped leaves grow at the base of the stem and smaller leaves intertwine with flowers on the upper stem. Found in wet meadows and wet open woods.

FLOWER: ²/₃"–1"   HEIGHT: 6"–25"   BLOOMS: July–Aug.

Small Purple-fringed Orchid
Platanthera psycodes

ORCHID FAMILY. Many fragrant rose-purple and white flowers alternate on a terminal spike. The prominent lip petal has three spreading fringed lobes and a backward pointing spur. Leaves are alternate, lance-shaped, and become narrower toward the top of the stem. The individual flowers are smaller and more compactly arranged than on the closely related large purple-fringed orchid. This native orchid grows in colonies in moist wet meadows, in bogs and on riverbanks.

FLOWER: 5/8"   **HEIGHT:** 2½'   **BLOOMS:** June–Aug.

Wild Lupine

Lupinus perennis

PEA/BEAN FAMILY. Vertical spikes of purple to pinkish-white pea flowers are found over palmately-divided stemmed leaves composed of seven to eleven oval to lance-shaped smooth edged leaflets. The only lupine native to the Eastern United States and the White Mountains, its flowers are sparsely spaced on the vertical stem when compared with the Garden Lupine. This rare species is considered threatened in New Hampshire and should not be disturbed because it is the sole host of the endangered Blue Karner Butterfly.

FLOWER: ½"–1"   **HEIGHT:** 8"–24"   **BLOOMS:** April–July

Garden Lupine   *Lupinus polyphyllus*

PEA/BEAN FAMILY. Pod-like blue (sometimes pink, white, or yellow) pea flowers appear in vertical spike-like columns over palmately-compound sets of eleven to seventeen leaflets. Originally a native of western U.S., it is seen in fields, meadows and along highways where it is planted as an ornamental or has escaped from gardens. Considered invasive by some, it forms large colonies which spread by rhizomes. Its seeds and pods (which resemble garden peas) are poisonous. Lupine carries a fungus which causes the livestock disease lupinosis.

FLOWER: ½"–1"   **HEIGHT:** 2'–4'   **BLOOMS:** May–July

Alfalfa
Medicago sativa

PEA/BEAN FAMILY. Blue-violet tightly packed short clusters of pea flowers sit atop the branched stalks of this widespread legume. Pinnately compound leaves composed of three leaflets, toothed at their tips, alternate up the stem. This native plant is found in sandy well-drained soil and is planted in fields by farmers for livestock silage. A rich source of protein, vitamins and calcium, Alfalfa is eaten by livestock, wildlife and people.

FLOWER: 1"–1¼"   **HEIGHT:** 3'   **BLOOMS:** June–Sept.

Pickerel Weed

Pontederia cordata

PICKEREL WEED FAMILY. Dense terminal clusters of bluish-purple flowers grow from the underwater creeping rhizomes of this aquatic plant. Flowers have two three-lobed lips. The upper lip has a distinct yellow spot. Beneath the flower cluster is a sheath-like bract, which wraps around the erect flower stem. A large heart-shaped, stalked, pointed leaf appears at the base of the plant. This native flower is found in still waters of wetlands and is an important food source for white tailed deer, wood ducks and muskrats.

FLOWER: ³/₈"   **HEIGHT:** 1'–2'   **BLOOMS:** June–Nov.

Ragged Robin

Lychnis flos-cuculi

PINK FAMILY. Numerous pink to white five-petalled flowers appear in terminal branching clusters. Each petal is dissected into four finger-shaped segments, two large fingers and two smaller ones, creating its "ragged" appearance. The upper stem is sticky and the lower stem is downy. Leaves are opposite, narrow and lance-shaped and they grow progressively larger toward the base of the stem. This naturalized flower, also known as "Cuckoo Flower," is found in moist areas of meadows, fields and at the sides of roads.

FLOWER: ½"   HEIGHT: 1'–3'   BLOOMS: May–July

Water Avens
Geum rivale

ROSE FAMILY. Long-stalked bristly nodding flowers have five pointed narrow purple sepals and five shorter pale yellow petals surrounding numerous stamens. Upper leaves are simple or lobed and alternate on a hairy stem; stalked compound lower leaves are composed of toothed leaflets; smaller, bract-like leaves grow in between. This native flower is found in wet meadows, bogs and marshes. Colonials and Native Americans made a medicinal drink that tasted like chocolate from its rhizome, hence the folk name "Indian Cocoa."

FLOWER: ½"–1"   **HEIGHT:** 10"–15"   **BLOOMS:** May–July

Nightshade
Solanum dulcamara

TOMATO/NIGHTSHADE FAMILY. Branched clusters of drooping blue-violet flowers grow from a climbing vine. Flowers have a five-lobed corolla with the petals curling back and a yellow cone-like center formed from five stamens that surround the pistil. Stalked alternate leaves are oval and pointed and some have small leaflets at their base. This naturalized European immigrant contains the alkaloid solanine, making its red berries and leaves highly poisonous. Found in moist areas of thickets, in disturbed ground and along shaded roads.

FLOWER: ½"   HEIGHT: 2'–8' vine   BLOOMS: May–Sept.

Blue Vervain

Verbena hastata

VERVAIN FAMILY. Pointed, spike-like elongated clusters of numerous tiny blue-purple flowers bloom from the bottom upward. Flowers are a funnel-shaped five-lobed corolla with four stamens and one pistil. Leaves are opposite, toothed, lance-shaped and grow up squarish stems. In ancient times it was used medicinally because it was thought to be a cure-all. This native flower is found in wet areas of thickets, at edges of streams and along country roads.

FLOWER: 1/8"   **HEIGHT:** 2'–6'   **BLOOMS:** July–Aug.

Cow Vetch

Vicia cracca

VETCH FAMILY. Violet-blue pea flowers in one-sided terminal clusters occur on thin arching stems. Pinnate compound leaves are composed of twelve or more opposite leaflets: the terminal leaflet forms a clasping tendril that helps this climbing vine surmount surrounding vegetation. This naturalized European vine is now an important food source for small mammals, birds and livestock.

FLOWER: ½"   **HEIGHT:** 2'–3'   **BLOOMS:** May–July

Dog Violet

Viola conspersa

VIOLET FAMILY. Light blue-purple flowers with dark veins on the lower petal and light beards on the side petals. A "stemmed" violet, its flower and leaves appear on separate stalks which branch off from the plant's main stem. Leaves are heart-shaped and finely toothed. This native violet is found in moist meadows and damp woods. It was used by Native Americans to make a medicinal tea to treat chest and heart pains.

FLOWER: ³/₄"   **HEIGHT:** 2"–8"   **BLOOMS:** March–July

Marsh Blue Violet   *Viola cucullata*

VIOLET FAMILY. This native "stemless violet" is characterized by its size (large for a wild violet) and its late bloom time. Petals are pale blue to purple. The two lateral petals have club-tipped beards and there is a small round whitish spur at the rear. The flower stalks have minute bracts halfway up. The leaves, on separate stalks, are heart-shaped and shallowly toothed. This summer violet is found in wet shaded sites in bogs, seeps, marshes and near ponds and streams.

FLOWER: ³⁄₄"–1"   **HEIGHT:** 6"–10"   **BLOOMS:** June–July

Northern Downy Violet   *Viola fimbriatula*

VIOLET FAMILY. A spurred "stemless" violet with light blue petals that fade to white at their base. Distinctive broadly lance-shaped leaves and leaflets grow in a dense low tuft. Leaves and stems are finely haired. The flower has beards on all three lower petals. The separate flower stalk rises above the leaves slightly. This low-lying native violet is found in dry fields and sandy soils.

FLOWER: ¹/₂"   **HEIGHT:** 4"–6"   **BLOOMS:** April–May

Common Blue Violet   *Viola papilionacea*

VIOLET FAMILY. A blue-purple "stemless" violet with flowers and leaves growing on separate stalks. Flower head generally rises above heart-shaped, toothed oval leaves. The bottom petals are deeply veined. Side petals have fine dense hairs (beards) near the center. Highly variable in appearance with many varieties identified in the Northeast. This native flower is found in meadows and moist woods. Its roots are a favorite food of the wild turkey.

FLOWER: ½"–1"   HEIGHT: 3"–8"   BLOOMS: April–May

Wooly Blue Violet   *Viola sororia*

VIOLET FAMILY. Purple-blue, small "stemless" native violet with prominent dark blue veins on the lower three petals. Lower petal has a rounded spur which protrudes backward over a curved, slightly hairy flower stalk. The side petals are prominently bearded and all the petals fade to white at their base. Sepals are oval, pointed and finely haired. Oval to heart shaped leaves on separate stems; stems and leaves are slightly hairy. Found on humus mats on wet rocky ledges, in enriched damp woods and at the edges of moist meadows.

FLOWER: ½"   **HEIGHT:** 3"–6"   **BLOOMS:** May–June

Northern Waterleaf
Hydrophyllum virginianum

WATERLEAF FAMILY. Pale blue-violet or white nodding, bell-shaped five-lobed corolla flowers grow in a dense terminal cluster. Five stamens with hairy filaments extend below the corolla's petal lobes. Leaves, pinnately divided into five or more lance-shaped sharply toothed leaflets, alternate on a hairy upper stem and appear water-stained, hence the common name. This threatened native flower grows in colonies and is found in rich moist woods and clearings.

FLOWER: ¼"–½" **HEIGHT:** 1'–2½' **BLOOMS:** May–Aug

Orange Hawkweed   *Hieracium aurantiacum*

ASTER FAMILY. Brilliant orange rays with yellow centers appear in clusters atop hairy leafless stalks. Numerous hairy basal leaves form a rosette on the ground. This flower spreads by downy windblown seeds and ground runners. An important wildlife food source, its leaves and seeds are eaten by birds and mammals. This naturalized European flower thrives in poor soil and is found in fields, pastures, and mountainsides.

FLOWER: ³/₄"   **HEIGHT:** 1'–2'   **BLOOMS:** June–Sept.

Day Lily

Hemerocallis fulva

LILY FAMILY. Flowers have three large orange petals with wavy edges and three similar sepals with slightly smoother edges. Flowers face upward atop tall leafless stalks. Tall narrow basal leaves are one to three feet high. Although not generally considered naturalized, this European garden flower often continues to grow without additional cultivation near old foundations, in abandoned gardens, on roadsides and in meadows. The common name comes from each flower lasting one day before wilting.

FLOWER: 3½"–5"   **HEIGHT:** 2'–4'   **BLOOMS:** May–June

Wood Lily *Lilium philadelphicum*

LILY FAMILY. One to five scarlet-orange, funnel-shaped flowers face upward atop thin erect stems. Three petals and three petal-like sepals are spotted brown at their base. Three to six lance-shaped leaves appear in whorls on its stalk. This showy native flower is found in dry sandy woods and pastures. Native Americans prepared its bulbs for food.

FLOWERS: 2" **HEIGHT:** 1'–3' **BLOOMS:** June–Aug.

Spotted Touch-me-not   *Impatiens capensis*

TOUCH-ME-NOT FAMILY. An orange trumpet-shaped flower with reddish-brown spots and a curved rear spur hangs from a thin stalk. The upper petal forms a hood over the two lower petals which hang down, forming a lip. Leaves are alternate, oval, thin, and have a pale underside. The seeds are a major food source for birds and bears. Hummingbirds are attracted to its nectar. Used by Native Americans to soothe the itch of insect bites and Poison Ivy. This native plant can grow in thick stands in shaded woods and open wetlands.

FLOWER: 1"   **HEIGHT:** 2'–5'   **BLOOMS:** June–Sept.

Nodding Burr Marigold   *Bidens cernua*

ASTER FAMILY. This composite flower has a large central disk of many small yellow flowers surrounded by a ring of short oval rays and pointed green sepal-like bracts. As the bloom ages it tends to nod toward earth. Leaves are opposite, narrow and lance-shaped with coarse saw-toothed edges. This native aster is found near streams, ponds and in low moist areas.

FLOWER: 1"–2" head   **HEIGHT:** 1'–3'   **BLOOMS:** Aug.–Oct.

Lance-leaved Coreopsis *Coreopsis lanceolata*

ASTER FAMILY. A showy composite flower made up of distinctive, notched, petal-shaped outer florets and inner florets compressed into a yellow disk. A good example of composite flowers that have evolved to mimic the showy petals of simple flowers. Leaves are lance to spatula-shaped, and appear opposite on a smooth stem. Found in dry fields and along country roads and highways. This naturalized flower escaped from colonial gardens.

FLOWER: 2"–2½"   **HEIGHT:** 1'–2'   **BLOOMS:** May–Oct.

57

Lance-leaved Goldenrod

Euthamia graminifolia

ASTER FAMILY. Small yellow cup-shaped flowers are arranged in a distinctive flat topped compound cluster above branching stems and stalk. Leaves are very narrow, smooth-edged, and lance-shaped. Found in moist to dry fields, in meadows and in bushy thickets. This beautiful fragrant native flower is needlessly avoided by allergy sufferers because of the mistaken belief that its pollen is dispersed by wind.

FLOWER: ¼"   **HEIGHT:** 1'–3'   **BLOOMS:** July–Oct.

Woodland Sunflower *Helianthus divaricatus*

ASTER FAMILY. One to a few yellow disk flowers, each with nine to fifteen rays, are found on a branched upper stem. Leaves are short-stalked or stalkless, opposite, oval to lance-shaped and toothed. The leaves' upper sides are rough and the undersides hairy. This native sunflower is found near shady woodland borders and in thickets. The plant's roots, flower buds and seeds were used by Native Americans for food and are a favorite food of woodland mammals and birds.

FLOWER: 2"–4" head   **HEIGHT:** 3'–7'   **BLOOMS:** Aug.–Sept.

Yellow Hawkweed   *Hieracium caespitosum*

ASTER FAMILY. Also known as King Devil, its flowers are composed of bright yellow rays with finely notched tips appearing in clusters atop leafless stalks. Distinctive black hairs are seen near base of flowers. Oblong, hairy, untoothed leaves form a rosette at the base of the tall stalk. Named after a European traditional belief that hawks ate the plant to improve their vision. This naturalized European species thrives in poor soil and is found in dry fields and pastures.

FLOWER: 1"–2"   **HEIGHT:** 1'–3'   **BLOOMS:** May–Aug.

Round-leaved Ragwort   *Packera obováta*

ASTER FAMILY. Flat-topped terminal clusters of golden-yellow daisy-like flower heads, each with seven to ten petal-like rays surround a disk of tiny tube flowers. Alternate basal leaves are toothed or toothless with an abruptly tapered base. Upper leaves can be divided into few or many parts. This endangered native flower is found in moist woods, bogs and swamps. All ragworts are toxic to livestock and humans.

FLOWER: ³/₄"   **HEIGHT:** 6"–24"   **BLOOMS:** April–June

61

Robbins Ragwort   *Packera schweinitziana*

ASTER FAMILY. Daisy-like, golden-yellow flower heads with eight to ten rays sit in a flat-topped terminal cluster. Basal leaves are heart-shaped, long-stalked and toothed. Upper leaves are pinnately lobed. Found in wet swamps, bogs and in moist woods. This native plant is known to be toxic to livestock and humans.

FLOWER: ³⁄₄"   **HEIGHT:** 6"–30"   **BLOOMS:** April–July

Black-eyed Susan   *Rudbeckia hirta*

ASTER FAMILY. This native coneflower is daisy-like in appearance, with bright yellow rays surrounding a purple-brown cone-shaped center disk. The solitary flower sits atop a rough bristly stem. Leaves beneath the flower head are small, pointed, oval and hairy. Basal leaves are larger and have three prominent veins. This favorite wildflower is seen in meadows, fields and on highway embankments. Seeds from this flower are a valuable source of food for birds during the winter.

FLOWER: 2"–3"   **HEIGHT:** 1'–3'   **BLOOMS:** June–Oct.

Tall Coneflower
Rudbeckia laciniata

ASTER FAMILY. Large attractive flower heads sit atop a very tall, smooth, branching stem. The center of the flower head is composed of many small perfect yellow-green disk flowers bunched into a round ball. Beneath the disk flowers are petal-like yellow rays that droop down. Small sepal-like bracts are found beneath the rays. Leaves are three-lobed, widely spaced, and alternate. This native perennial Aster is found near streams, ponds, in wet meadows and in open wet woodlands.

FLOWER: 1"–4"   **HEIGHT:** 3'–6'   **BLOOMS:** July–Sept.

Coneflower

Rudbeckia speciosa

ASTER FAMILY. These variably-colored relatives of the native Black-eyed Susan are western American wildflowers introduced to this area as roadside ornamental plants. Many varieties of coneflower are visible in late summer along highways and fields. Although not generally considered naturalized in New Hampshire, they are occasionally seen where planted in fields and pastures.

FLOWER: 2"–5"   HEIGHT: 1'–2'   BLOOMS: July–Sept.

Canadian Goldenrod   *Solidago canadensis*

ASTER FAMILY. Numerous perfectly formed bright yellow miniature flowers arch from flower stalks in dense one-sided terminal plumes. Below the inflorenscence is an unbranched stem, the upper part being hairy. Leaves are alternate, narrow, and lance-shaped with three prominent veins and sharp teeth. This native goldenrod is found in overgrown fields, in meadows and along country roads.

FLOWER: ⅛"   HEIGHT: 2'–5'   BLOOMS: July–Sept.

Rough-stemmed Goldenrod *Solidago rugosa*

ASTER FAMILY. Hundreds of small yellow flowers each with a disk and six to eleven rays form arching plumes on branches near the top of this plant. Pointed, oval, toothed leaves with a prominent central vein alternate up the stem. Leaves, branches and stem are hairy. This native goldenrod often blooms in the vicinity of ragweed, whose allergy-causing airborne pollen is mistakenly thought to come from the nearby Goldenrod. Found in fields, in meadows, at woodland edges and along country roads.

FLOWER: ⅛"   **HEIGHT:** 2'–5'   **BLOOMS:** July–Sept.

Common Tansy

Tanacetum vulgare

Aster family. Flat-topped clusters of deep yellow disk flowers appear like golden buttons on this common perennial. Leaves are alternate, toothed, aromatic and pinnately divided one to two times. This escaped European garden flower is found near old foundations, at field edges and roadsides. Colonial Americans used the flower heads and young leaves as a sage substitute. Mature leaves and stems are now known to be poisonous due to their tanacerum content.

Flower: 1/2" **Height:** 2'–3' **Blooms:** July–Sept.

Common Dandelion *Taraxacum officinale*

ASTER FAMILY. This prolific flower is common throughout the world. Its single composite flower head with numerous ragged tipped rays sits atop a long stalk. Long oval basal leaves with deep triangular notches give the appearance of "lions" teeth. The leaves of this naturalized Eurasian aster were used by colonists for salad greens and, when dried and ground, as a substitute for coffee. The flower heads were also fermented to produce wine.

FLOWER: ½"–2"   **HEIGHT:** 2"–18"   **BLOOMS:** April–Sept.

Colt's Foot
Tussilago farfara

ASTER FAMILY. A yellow composite flower with many layered thin rays surrounding a yellow center disk sits atop a scaly reddish-gray stalk. Large fragrant leaves, shaped like a "colt's foot," appear later. This naturalized European species propagates rapidly through rhizomes. It is extremely invasive and can compete aggressively against native plants where it is found. Its former "traditional" use as an herbal cough medicine was discontinued when Colt's Foot was found to contain liver toxin.

FLOWER: 1" **HEIGHT:** 3"–18" **BLOOMS:** April–May

Horned Bladderwort   *Utricularia cornuta*

BLADDERWORT FAMILY. One to five bright yellow flowers have a two-lipped corolla. The lower lip is bonnet-shaped and has a backward-curved spur. This native carnivorous plant lives in the wet acidic peaty soils of bogs. The underground leaves are delicate and have syringe-like bladders that trap and digest small organisms. Seen growing near Sundew and Pitcher Plants.

FLOWER: ³/₄"   **HEIGHT:** 2"–12"   **BLOOMS:** June–Sept.

Common Bladderwort *Utricularia macrorhiza*

BLADDERWORT FAMILY. Yellow flowers on reddish stalks are found singly or in clusters on stems which rise from the water. This aquatic bladderwort has a two-lipped corolla and a spur beneath. The leaves of this native carnivorous plant are finely divided and float in a tangled mat just beneath the water surface. Bladders on the leaves have concave haired sides which trap the aquatic organisms the plant feeds on. Found in quiet waters of ponds, bogs and marshes.

FLOWER: ³/₄"   **HEIGHT:** 1 ¹/₂"–8"   **BLOOMS:** June–Sept.

Marsh Marigold   *Caltha palustris*

Buttercup family. Our largest native member of the buttercup family, this shiny yellow flower appears in carpet-like colonies in wet woods, streambanks and marshy areas. Five or more, bright-yellow, petal-like sepals surround numerous orange tinged stamens and pistils. Large, lance-shaped, toothed leaves are seen underneath flowers. Although the leaves of this plant have historically been cooked as greens, they contain the poison protoanemonin and must be cooked thoroughly, with several water changes, to avoid toxic effects.

Flower: 1"–5"   **Height:** 6"–12"   **Blooms:** April–June

Kidney-leaf Buttercup *Ranunculus abortivus*

BUTTERCUP FAMILY. This small, yellow, five-petalled, inconspicuous flower bears little resemblance to other buttercups. Flowers have five yellow petal-like sepals surrounding short undeveloped petals with numerous pistils and stamens. Flower sits on a stalked branching stem. Kidney-shaped basal leaves have scalloped edges. Oblong upper leaves are lobed, unstalked, and appear in bunches near the flowers. This native plant is found in fields, meadows and open woods.

FLOWER: ¹/₄ "   **HEIGHT:** 6"–24"   **BLOOMS:** April–Aug.

Common Buttercup   *Ranunculus acris*

BUTTERCUP FAMILY. This plant's bright shiny yellow flowers can occur singly or in axial clusters. It has five spreading sepals, five petals and numerous stamens and pistils. Stalks are tall and hairy. Basal leaves have three to seven deeply divided lobes while the smaller upper leaves have three segments. This acidic plant is avoided by livestock because it causes external and internal blistering. This widespread naturalized buttercup is seen in open fields, meadows and disturbed areas.

FLOWER: 1"   **HEIGHT:** 2'–3'   **BLOOMS:** May–Sept.

Wild Parsnip   *Pastinaca sativa*

CARROT/PARSLEY FAMILY. Numerous small yellow flowers sit in clusters atop ridged branched stems. Leaves are alternate, and pinnately compound, composed of five to fifteen sharp-toothed leaflets. Cultivated for hundreds of years, this naturalized European flower escaped from colonial herb gardens. Found in old fields, meadows, pastures and roadsides. Wet leaves cause allergic dermatitis if touched.

FLOWER: ¼"   **HEIGHT:** 2'–6'   **BLOOMS:** May–Aug.

Golden Alexanders

Zizia aurea

CARROT/PARSLEY FAMILY. Numerous, deep yellow, five-petalled flowers sit in terminal clusters (two to four inches wide) atop branching flower stalks which grow from a central vertical stem. Finely toothed leaves alternate on the stem. Upper leaves are composed of three lance-shaped leaflets. Lower leaves are larger and twice compound (composed of three sets of three leaflets). This early spring native can be found in wet and dry woodlands, in fields and near stream beds.

FLOWER: 2"–4"   HEIGHT: 1'–3'   BLOOMS: April–June

Evening Primrose   *Oenothera biennis*

Evening Primrose family. One of many similar species of showy flowers that open in the evening and wilt in sunshine. Flowers have four yellow petals and a stigma with a cross-shaped tip. Flowers are arranged in axial clusters on short stems or appear as a solitary flower. This native herb is found in dry fields and meadows. It was one of the first plants to be exported from North America to Europe because of its reputation as an effective treatment for whooping cough.

Flower: 1"–2"   **Height:** 1'–3'   **Blooms:** June–Sept.

Sundrops   *Oenothera perennis*

EVENING PRIMROSE FAMILY. This day blooming evening primrose has yellow flower heads with four notched petals and four sepals. The cross-shaped stigma is surrounded by eight orange stamens. Lance-like, sharply pointed, smooth edged leaves appear opposite on a purple tinged hairy stalk. This native primrose is found in meadows, fields and open woods. Seeds of this flower are a valuable source of food for birds.

FLOWER: 1"–2"   **HEIGHT:** 1'–3'   **BLOOMS:** June–Sept.

Butter and Eggs

Linaria vulgaris

FIGWORT FAMILY. Terminal clusters have pale yellow flowers with upper and lower lips closed together. A distinctive orange mark is seen on the upper side of the bright yellow lower lip. Long, narrow, alternative leaves appear on smooth vertical stalks below the flowers. The lips of this flower are forced open by bumblebees seeking a nectar pool contained in the downward-pointed spur at the bottom of the flower. This naturalized European flower grows in poor soil, dry fields and disturbed areas.

FLOWER: 1"   **HEIGHT:** 1'–3'   **BLOOMS:** May–Oct.

Muskflower
Mimulus moschatus

FIGWORT FAMILY. Small yellow tube-shaped flowers appear on short stalks in leaf axils along a vertical stem. The petals are fused into a corolla tube with five lobes. Four hairy yellow stamens are attached to the inner sides of the corolla tube. Leaves are oval to lance shaped with short stalks. Both the leaves and the stem are very hairy. This native perennial herb is considered endangered in New Hampshire. It is found along streams, at pond edges and in roadside seeps.

FLOWER: ½"–¾"   **HEIGHT:** 8"–20"   **BLOOMS:** June–Sept.

Yellow Rattle

Rhinanthus crista-galli

FIGWORT FAMILY. Yellow flowers form a spike-like cluster on one side of a vertical stem. The flower is composed of a large round flattened green calyx with two-lipped yellow petals protruding from its tip. The lower lip has three lobes while the upper lip forms a hood. Leaves are sharply pointed and sharply toothed. Seeds rattle in the calyx when the mature plant is shaken. This uncommon native flower is semi-parasitic, supplementing photosynthesis by feeding off the roots of nearby plants. It is found in fields, meadows and along roads.

FLOWER: ½"–1"   **HEIGHT:** 6"–3'   **BLOOMS:** June–Sept.

Common Mullein *Verbascum thapsus*

FIGWORT FAMILY. Club-shaped vertical clusters of yellow flowers are arranged atop thick hairy stalks with alternating flannel-like leaves. Flower petals are fused in a corolla with five uneven-lengthed lobes. Five stamens are also unequal; the upper three are short, the lower two are long. Leaves of this naturalized European flower were used by colonists and Native Americans as insulation for shoes and clothes. Leaves were also used since Roman times to make a cough remedy and anti-itch balm. Found in dry rocky soils and on hillsides.

FLOWER: ³/₄"–1"   **HEIGHT:** 2'–7'   **BLOOMS:** June–Sept.

Yellow Flag Iris · *Iris pseudacorus*

IRIS FAMILY. Showy yellow flowers with three petal-like downward-curved sepals, three upward-curved petals, and three stamens, sit atop erect stalks. Narrow sword-shaped deep green leaves rise above the flowers. This flower is increasingly found along stream borders, pond edges and in marshy areas. A naturalized European garden flower, it escaped cultivation after introduction and is considered highly invasive.

FLOWER: 3"   **HEIGHT:** 2'–3'   **BLOOMS:** June–July

Clintonia   *Clintonia borealis*

LILY FAMILY. Nodding clusters of greenish yellow flowers occur atop long leafless stalks over two to five shiny oblong basal leaves. Also called "Blue Bead Lily" because it bears deep blue berries. This native New Hampshire lily is found in mountainous regions, moist woodlands and bogs.

FLOWER: ³/₄"   **HEIGHT:** 6"–16"   **BLOOMS:** May–June

Trout Lily
Erythronium americanum

LILY FAMILY. Each plant has a solitary, bright yellow, nodding flower with petal-like sepals that curve distinctly backward showing red-brownish anthers. Named Trout Lily because its mottled brown and purplish lanceolate basal leaves resemble brown or brook trout. This native New Hampshire lily forms colonies in rich moist woodlands. Flowers close in bad weather.

FLOWER: 1"–1½"   HEIGHT: 6"–12"   BLOOMS: April–May

Canada Lily — *Lilium canadense*

Lily family. Large nodding yellow-orange flowers have three petals and three petal-like sepals, revealing red-brown tipped anthers underneath. Each flower hangs on its own leafless stalk that branches from the stem at the center of a whorl of four to ten lance-shaped leaves. A native flower, this lily is found in wet meadows and woodlands. Native Americans ate the roots and flower buds.

Flower: 2"–3"   **Height:** 2'–5'   **Blooms:** June–Aug.

Sessile-leaved Bellwort   *Uvularia sessilifolia*

LILY FAMILY. One or two creamy-yellow, slender drooping flowers have slightly re-curved pointed petal tips. Long narrow, alternate pointed leaves surround the flowers. This plant was once thought to be useful to treat throat disorders because the flower resembles the uvula of the human throat. This native New Hampshire member of the Lily family, also known as "Wild Oats" is found in moist shaded woodlands.

FLOWER: 1"   HEIGHT: 6"–12"   BLOOMS: April–June

Common Wintercress   *Barbarea vulgaris*

Mustard family. Flower heads with four petals in the shape of a cross form elongated terminal clusters. Basal leaves are pinnately divided into one to four pairs of lateral lobes and have short stalks. Upper leaves are lobed and clasp the stem. Naturalized from Europe, this early blooming mustard forms prominent patches of yellow in fields and along roads. European settlers cooked the young leaves as greens.

Flower: 1/4"–5/16"   **Height:** 1'–2'   **Blooms:** April–June

Yellow Lady's Slipper *Cypripedium pubescens*

ORCHID FAMILY. This flower has three petals and three sepals. The prominent yellow lower petal is slipper-shaped and the two lateral petals are distinctively spiraled. The upper sepal forms a hood over the yellow "slipper" petal and the two lower sepals are fused behind the "slipper." Large, deeply veined, oval to lance-shaped leaves alternate on a thick stalk. This rare native orchid, considered threatened in New Hampshire, is found in moist rich woodlands as well as dry hardwood forest sites.

FLOWER: 2"   **HEIGHT:** 8"–28"   **BLOOMS:** April–June

Birdsfoot Trefoil

Lotus corniculatus

Pea/Bean family. Bright yellow flowers in umbrella-shaped clusters appear on bare stems. Compound leaves are composed of five hairy oval leaflets, three in a clover-like arrangement on a short stem and two at the base of that stem. The common name is derived from the slender seed pods that appear in the shape of a "bird's foot." This naturalized European flower is in a symbiotic relationship with a nitrogen-fixing bacteria that increases the availability of nitrogen in the soil. This plant is also used for erosion control.

Flower: ½"   **Height:** 6"–24"   **Blooms:** June–Sept.

Hop Clover   *Trifolium aureum*

PEA/BEAN FAMILY. Forty to sixty small flowers appear in oval clusters atop smooth stalks which freely branch from a vertical main stem. Palmately compound leaves are composed of three finely toothed oval leaflets. When flower heads wither they turn brown and resemble "hops." This naturalized European clover is used as ground cover because of its symbiotic relationship with nitrogen-fixing bacteria that form the characteristic nodules of leguminous plants and thus enrich the soil. An important food source for small birds and mammals.

FLOWER: ¹/₄"   HEIGHT: 6"–8"   BLOOMS: June–Sept.

Celandine *Chelidonium majus*

POPPY FAMILY. This plant has a deep yellow flower with four or more slightly wrinkled oval petals and numerous yellow stamens. Flowers occur in loose clusters on hairy stems over deeply lobed leaves that are green on top and lighter on the underside. This naturalized European flower is considered an invasive species in the White Mountains. It is found in moist soil at the edges of woodlands, in fields and in pastures. Its sap and leaves are known to be toxic to animals and humans.

FLOWER: ½"–¾" **HEIGHT:** 1'–2' **BLOOMS:** May–Sept.

93

Fringed Loosestrife

Lysimachia ciliata

PRIMROSE FAMILY. Flowers have five yellow petals with spike-like teeth protruding from petal tips. Flowers, often nodding, hang on long stalks that emerge from the base of paired leaves. Leaves are lance-shaped near the stem top and oval-shaped at the plant's base. Native to New Hampshire, it is commonly found in damp woods, on floodplains, in swamps and streamsides.

FLOWER: ³/₄"   **HEIGHT:** 1' to 4'   **BLOOMS:** June–August

Garden Loosestrife   *Lysimachia punctata*

PRIMROSE FAMILY. Yellow flowers in vertical clusters
are seen bunched with whorls of oval to lance-shaped
leaves on hairy stems. Five pointed petals surround
an orange center with five prominent yellow stamens.
This naturalized flower from Europe escaped from
gardens. It is found along rivers, on floodplains and
in damp woods.

FLOWER: ³/₄"   **HEIGHT:** 2'–3'   **BLOOMS:** June–Aug.

Swamp Candles
Lysimachia terrestris

Primrose family. Spike-like vertical clusters of bright yellow flowers can dominate wetlands where this native flower grows. Flower has five petals, five sepals and five stamens. The small bright yellow pointed petals exhibit distinctive pairs of red dots at their base. Short sepals are pointed and stamens have prominent bean-shaped anthers. Leaves, usually in pairs, are found beneath the flower clusters. Found in marshes, moist thickets and low areas.

Flower: ½"   **Height:** 1'–3'   **Blooms:** June–Aug.

Yellow Avens

Geum aleppicum

ROSE FAMILY. Small flowers with five bright yellow widely spaced heart-shaped petals appear on separate short stalks branching from a central stem. Ten to twenty or more stamens surround a central dome-shaped yellow disk. Upper leaves are sharply toothed and unlobed. Lower leaves are compound, lobed and toothed. Both flower stalks and stem have firm erect hairs. This native rhizomatous herb is found in meadows, in thickets, at woodland openings and along country roads.

FLOWER: 7/8"   **HEIGHT:** 1'–3'   **BLOOMS:** May–July

Mountain Avens

Geum peckii

ROSE FAMILY. This plant has one or more yellow flowers, each with five notched petals. Lower leaves are large, alternate, and pinnately compound while upper leaves are smaller and unevenly toothed. In the fall, this plant is noted for its crimson-red foliage. This native flower is seen in the alpine regions of the White Mountains. Species name was given in memory of the early botanist William Peck. Mountain Avens is considered threatened in New Hampshire and imperiled globally.

FLOWER: 1"   HEIGHT: 6"–24"   BLOOMS: June–Aug.

Canadian Dwarf Cinquefoil

Potentilla canadensis

ROSE FAMILY. A single yellow flower with five petals on a long leafless stalk grows from the stem at the base of leaves. Leaves are palmately compound, with five leaflets. Unlike common cinquefoil, each leaflet is only toothed above the middle. This early blooming, low, spreading plant is found in dry fields and open woods. Tea from the bitter roots of this native flower was traditionally used as a mouthwash and gargle.

FLOWER: 1/2"–5/8" HEIGHT: 2"–6" BLOOMS: April–June

Rough-fruited Cinquefoil   *Potentilla recta*

ROSE FAMILY. Five pale sulfur-yellow petals around an orange center give this tall erect plant its folk name "sulfer cinquefoil." Each petal is notched and is slightly longer than the five narrow, pointed green sepals. Flowers with numerous pistils and stamens appear in clusters on a hairy stalk. Leaves are palmately divided into five to seven blunt-tipped, toothed leaflets. This naturalized species is considered invasive and is kept away from livestock because it contains toxic compounds.

FLOWER: ¾"   **HEIGHT:** 1'–2'   **BLOOMS:** May–Aug.

Old-Field (Common) Cinquefoil
Potentilla simplex

ROSE FAMILY. Yellow, five-petalled flowers grow on slightly hairy stalks that branch from main stems near upper leaves. Leaves are palmately divided and composed of five oblong to lance-shaped, fully toothed leaflets that alternate on reddish, slightly hairy, trailing stems. This common New Hampshire native has little known food value and thrives in worn-out, dry acidic soil, in abandoned pastures and in open woods.

FLOWER: ¹⁄₄"–¹⁄₂"   HEIGHT: 3"–24"   BLOOMS: June–July

Barren Strawberry · *Waldsteinia fragarioides*

ROSE FAMILY. Several small yellow five-petalled flowers with five sepals and numerous stamens form a terminal cluster on this strawberry-like woodland evergreen. This creeping plant has compound basal leaves with three toothed leaflets. An endangered native of New Hampshire's thickets, woods and fields. Called "False Strawberry" because it looks similar to the wild strawberry plant except that it has yellow, not white petals and it bears relatively large, inedible fruit.

FLOWER: 1/2"   **HEIGHT:** 3"–8"   **BLOOMS:** April–June

Common St. John's Wort

Hypericum perforatum

St. John's Wort family. Flower has five bright yellow petals with perforated tips and black dots near the petal edges. Numerous stamens have clearly defined small round anthers on their tips. Simple leaves are elliptical to oblong in shape, opposite on the stem, and have translucent dots. This naturalized herb was used during the Middle Ages as an anti-anxiety tonic. It is named after St. John because it was traditionally thought to bloom on St. John's Eve, June 24th.

Flower: ³/₄"–1" **Height:** 1'–2¹/₂' **Blooms:** June–Sept.

Smooth Yellow Violet

Viola pubescens var. scabriuscula

VIOLET FAMILY. A small yellow violet with dark veins on petals near the center of the flower and hairless leaves and stems. A "stemmed violet," its flower and leaves are on separate short stalks. Heart-shaped leaves with rounded teeth appear at or near the height of the flower head. Small, smooth, untoothed leaflets mark where the leaf and flower stalks branch off from the central stem. This native violet is found in meadows and moist woods.

FLOWER: ³/₈"–¹/₂"   **HEIGHT:** 4"–12"   **BLOOMS:** April–May

Downy Yellow Violet

Viola pubescens var. pubescens

VIOLET FAMILY. A small yellow "stemmed violet" with fine hair on leaves, stipules, stalks, stem and sepals. Lower petal has dark veins and lateral petals have small yellow beards. Sepals are small, oval to lance-shaped and hidden behind petals. Leaves are heart-shaped with rounded toothed edges. Small finely toothed stipules occur where the flower stalk meets the leaf stalk. This native violet is similar to the smooth yellow violet except for the fine hair on most of the plant.

FLOWER: ½"–⅝"　**HEIGHT:** 6"–8"　**BLOOMS:** April–May

Round-leaved Yellow Violet
Viola rotundifolia

VIOLET FAMILY. A "stemless" native violet, it is our only yellow violet having flowers and leaves growing on individual stalks. The bright yellow five-petalled flower has purple veins on its lower petals. Two to five round-ish basal leaves show many teeth. This violet is vegetatively inconspicuous with leaves that often lay flat on the ground or under leaf litter. Found in deep woods, near stones and tree trunks.

FLOWER: 3/4"–1"   HEIGHT: 2"–5"   BLOOMS: April–May

Yellow Pond Lily   *Nuphar variegata*

WATER-LILY FAMILY. An aquatic flower, sometimes red-tinged, with five to six bright yellow petal-like sepals, many smaller petals, numerous stamens and greenish pistils. Flowers float above veined heart-shaped leaves. Plants die back in the fall creating rich organic matter in ponds. Seeds of this native water lily are a food source for waterfowl and marsh birds. Native Americans ground and roasted the seeds and boiled the roots like potatoes.

FLOWER: 1½"–2½"   **HEIGHT:** 4"–1' above water
BLOOMS: June–Sept.

107

Yellow Wood Sorrel   *Oxalis stricta*

WOOD SORREL FAMILY. A delicate yellow flower with
five petals and ten stamens. Its leaves are palmately
divided forming heart-shaped, clover-like leaflets that
close at night. This native flower is commonly seen in
colonies in moist woods, cultivated fields and open
places. Although the leaves have been used as salad
greens, this sour tasting plant is potentially poisonous
if eaten in large quantities due to the presence of oxalic acid.

FLOWER: 1/4"–1/2"   **HEIGHT:** 4"–12"   **BLOOMS:** May–Sept.

Wild Calla Lily   *Calla palustris*

ARUM FAMILY. A wide white spathe with a pointed tip and rolled edges surrounds a spadix of tiny yellow flowers. Leaves are large, long-stalked, shiny, oblong, and heart-shaped. This water arum forms a cluster of red berries that are a food source of birds and small mammals. Native to New Hampshire's shallow waters and wetlands.

FLOWER: 1"–2"   **HEIGHT:** 6"–12"   **BLOOMS:** May–Aug.

Yarrow   *Achillea millefolium*

ASTER FAMILY. Dozens of small white flowers form Yarrow's flat-topped terminal clusters. Each minute flower has a central disk surrounded by four to six rays. Tall, erect, hairy stems have alternating fern-like leaves. Seen in meadows, near old fields and on hillsides up into the alpine zone. This aromatic naturalized European herb was used by colonists and Native Americans to reduce fever and to treat skin disorders. Said to have been discovered by the Greek hero, Achilles, and thus its Latin genus name "Achillea."

FLOWER: ¼"   **HEIGHT:** 1'–3'   **BLOOMS:** June–Sept.

Pearly Everlasting · *Anaphalis margaritacea*

ASTER FAMILY. Twelve or more pearly white flower heads arranged in branched terminal clusters lie on top of erect, finely haired stems. Leaves are narrow and alternate, with a wooly underside. This New Hampshire native flower is located in dry areas of meadows and pasturelands. Butterflies and moths are needed to pollinate its flowers because its pistil and its stamens are on separate plants. Now a favorite dried flower, Native Americans once used the plant to treat paralysis and soothe coughs.

FLOWER: 1/4"   **HEIGHT:** 1'–3'   **BLOOMS:** July–Sept.

Plantain-leaved Pussytoes

Antennaria plantaginifolia

ASTER FAMILY. Small terminal clusters of soft fuzzy white florets sit atop a scaly leatherish stem. Rosettes of grayish, veined, oval leaves form at the base of the flowers' stem. The emerging flower heads are said to resemble the fur and toes of "pussy cats" hence the common name. This native flower appears in large colonies and spreads through a system of runners. Found in open woodlands, in fields and meadows where its blanket-like stands of white flowers are said to signal the winter's end.

FLOWER: ³/₈" clusters   **HEIGHT:** 3"–4"   **BLOOMS:** April–June

White Wood Aster

Aster divaricatus

ASTER FAMILY. Composite flower heads appear in branched open clusters on upper stems over broad, heart-shaped, saw-toothed leaves. A central disk composed of many small, yellow, five-lobed tube flowers is surrounded by oblong white ray flowers. This small native aster is found in dry to moist rich soils of open woodlands and in forest clearings.

FLOWER: ¾" head   **HEIGHT:** 2'–3'   **BLOOMS:** July–Oct.

Oxeye Daisy   *Chrysanthemum leucanthemum*

ASTER FAMILY: This common naturalized flower is composed of hundreds of small disk flowers compressed into a bright yellow disk with a dimpled center. The white petal-like rays that surround the central disk are leaves that have evolved to mimic the petals of simple flowers. Leaves are simple, oblong, alternate and toothed. The name "daisy" is from ancient English for "day's eye" referring to the central sun-like disk. Daisies cause an unpleasant flavor in cow's milk. Widely found in meadows and along country roads.

FLOWER: 1"–2" disk   HEIGHT: 1'–3'   BLOOMS: June–Aug.

Flat-topped White Aster
Doellingeria umbellata

ASTER FAMILY. Flower heads appear in closely spaced, flat-topped clusters atop tall, branched stems. This beautiful aster clearly illustrates the structure of compound flowers. In each flower head six to fifteen oblong white rays surround a dome-like bouquet of minute, five-lobed, perfectly formed yellow tube flowers. Long, lance-shaped, toothed, stalkless leaves are angled closely to sturdy stems. This native aster is found in moist areas.

FLOWER: ³/₄"   **HEIGHT:** 3'–7'   **BLOOMS:** August

Daisy Fleabane

Erigeron annuus

ASTER FAMILY. A compact disk of hundreds of yellow florets is surrounded by 50 to 100 short, white to pinkish-purple rays. This compound flower sits atop a stem with erect stiff hairs and lance-shaped leaves that are toothed near their middle. Named "fleabane" after the superstitious belief that hanging the dried flower heads inside would drive out fleas. This native flower is found in fields and meadows.

FLOWER: ½" disk　　**HEIGHT:** 1'–5'　　**BLOOMS:** June–Sept.

Common Fleabane   *Erigeron philadelphicus*

ASTER FAMILY. Similar to Daisy Fleabane except that its white to pink rays are thinner and more numerous (100 to 150). Its stem has soft hairs and arrow-shaped leaves, some of which may clasp the stem. This native New Hampshire member of the Aster family is found in open woods, fields and moist meadows. Settlers believed that dried flowers kept inside drove away fleas.

FLOWER: 1" disk   **HEIGHT:** 6"–36"   **BLOOMS:** May–August

Silverrod
Solidago bicolor

ASTER FAMILY. Miniature composite flowers are arranged in spread out spike-shaped clusters. Each flower has seven to nine silver rays surrounding a central disk. Flowers and leaves grow along a hairy stem. Lower leaves are alternate, stalked, oblong and toothed. Upper leaves are shorter, narrow and sometimes stalkless and toothless. This is the only goldenrod that is not yellow. Native to New Hampshire's woodlands and clearings, it is usually found growing in dry soil.

FLOWER: 1/4"   **HEIGHT:** 1'–3'   **BLOOMS:** July–Sept.

Spring Forget-me-not   *Myosotis verna*

Borage family. The White Mountains' native Forget-me-not! Small, white, funnel-shaped flowers with yellow centers appear along slightly curled branches. Leaves are stalkless, oblong and are closely angled to the erect hairy stem. Closely related to the naturalized True Forget-me-not, it has less curved flower branches, the flowers are smaller and more spread out, and the calyx is bristly. This native flower likes dry woods with rich soil. Often seen near stands of True Forget-me-nots.

Flower: 1/8"–1/4"   **Height:** 4"–16"   **Blooms:** April–June

One-flowered Cancer-root

Orobanche uniflora

BROOMRAPE FAMILY. One or more leafless stalks, each with a single tube flower, rise from a short underground stem. The flower's lavender-tinged white petaltubes have five lobes. The lower lobes have yellow beards. The leaves are reduced to small scales on the stem. This plant does not create food by photosynthesis. It obtains nourishment from the roots of plants nearby. This native flower is found in damp woods, near streams and along country roads.

FLOWER: ³/₄"   **HEIGHT:** 3"–10"   **BLOOMS:** May–June

White Baneberry
Actaea pachypoda

BUTTERCUP FAMILY. This flower's small white petals are overshadowed by numerous long stamens. It has a pronounced ovary that is topped off by a stigma of the same diameter. Flowers appear in distinctive globe-shaped terminal clusters on leafless stems. Leaves are divided into many toothed leaflets which generally appear some distance below the flower cluster. The poisonous "bane" berries mature to white with black dots, hence the folk name "doll's eyes." This native New Hampshire flower is found in rich moist woods.

FLOWER: ¹/₄"–²/₃"   **HEIGHT:** 1'–3'   **BLOOMS:** May–June

121

Red Baneberry

Actaea rubra

Buttercup family. Similar in appearance to White Baneberry, except that the diameter of the stigma is slightly less than that of the ovary and the plant bears red, not white, berries. Like the White Baneberry, the fruit is poisonous. Flowers appear in a globe-like cluster on a leafless stem. The divided leaves are composed of irregularly shaped, deeply toothed leaflets growing below the flowers. This New Hampshire native is found in rich moist woodlands.

Flower: ¼"–²/₃"   **Height:** 1'–3'   **Blooms:** May–June

Canada Anemone   *Anemone canadensis*

BUTTERCUP FAMILY. Terminal clusters have one to three white flowers. Each flower has five large oblong unequal petal-like sepals with numerous stamens. Flowers sit atop long stalks with a single pair of stalkless upper leaves and a whorl of three deeply lobed stalkless lower leaves. This native flower closes at night. Found in damp meadows, on river banks and in lakeside woodlands. Once used by Native Americans to dress wounds but now considered poisonous.

FLOWER: 1¼"   **HEIGHT:** 1'–2'   **BLOOMS:** May–July

123

Wood Anemone   *Anemone quinquefolia*

BUTTERCUP FAMILY. A solitary white flower sits atop a long stalk. Five petal-like sepals (petals are absent) surround many stamens and pistils. A whorl of three leaves, each of which is palmately divided into three to five lobes, surrounds the central stem. Colonies of this delicate New Hampshire native thrive in thickets, woods and woodland borders. The long-stalked flowers ripple with the wind giving rise to its folk name "Windflower."

FLOWER: 1"   **HEIGHT:** 4"–8"   **BLOOMS:** April–June

European Columbine   *Aquilegia vulgaris*

Buttercup family. This white to bluish purple flower has five distinctive, pointed petals with curved hollow spurs that extend over the rear of the flower. Unlike Wild Columbine, the stamens do not protrude beyond the petals. Compound leaves are composed of three deeply lobed leaflets. Pollinated by bumblebees, this naturalized European garden escapee is well established along fields and at the edges of woods.

Flower: 1"–2"   **Height:** 1'–2'   **Blooms:** April–May

125

Virgin's Bower
Clematis virginiana

BUTTERCUP FAMILY. This vine is known for its showy seed stage as seen in the photograph above. Long, soft, gray hairs grow from multifaceted seed capsules. The seed capsules develop from loose clusters of small white flowers with four to five petal-like sepals. Compound leaves are formed from three deeply toothed, oval, stalked leaflets. This New Hampshire native is found in moist woods, thickets, river and streambanks, and along roads.

SIZE: 2"–3" seed capsule   **HEIGHT:** 6'–10' vine
BLOOMS: July–Sept.

Goldthread — *Coptis trifolia*

CROWFOOT FAMILY. A solitary flower with five inward-curved petal-like sepals surrounding numerous fine stamens and five to eight globular yellow pistils sits atop a slender ringed leafless stalk. Evergreen basal leaves are palmately divided into three leaflets with scalloped-toothed edges. Named after its thread-like golden roots that were once used by Native Americans and settlers to treat canker sores. This native evergreen is found in mossy woods, bogs, and damp areas above the timberline.

FLOWER: ½"   **HEIGHT:** 3"–6"   **BLOOMS:** May–July

Tall Meadow-rue   *Thalictrum pubescens*

BUTTERCUP FAMILY. Many clusters of distinctive petal-less flowers with starry bursts of thread-like stamens. Small upper leaves are attached directly to the stem. The lower leaves are divided into three to seven lobed leaflets. This common fragrant flower attracts many bees and butterflies. A native New Hampshire herb, Tall Meadow-rue is found in open sunny wetlands, in meadows and along streamsides.

FLOWER: 1"　　**HEIGHT:** 3'–8'　　**BLOOMS:** July–Sept.

Bublet-bearing Water Hemlock

Cicuta bulbifera

CARROT/PARSLEY FAMILY. A close relative of this tiny flower became world famous as "poison hemlock" when the Greek philosopher Socrates drank a deadly tea made from its leaves rather than submit to the decrees of an unjust government. Clusters of small white flowers occur on a slender branching stem with very narrow pencil-shaped upper leaves. Lobed basal leaves are slightly wider. This extremely poisonous native herb is found in seeps, near river edges and near ponds.

FLOWER: 1/10"–1/8"　　**HEIGHT:** 1'–3'　　**BLOOMS:** June–Aug.

Queen Anne's Lace *Daucus carota*

CARROT/PARSLEY FAMILY. Many tiny five-petalled flowers in rounded to flat-topped clusters form lace-like patterns with distinctive spiny bracts below. Immature flower clusters are curled up resembling a bird's nest. Hairy stems have long alternate fern-like leaves. A carrot-like odor attracts bees and butterflies. Found in dry fields and meadows this naturalized European flower, also known as "Wild Carrot" was used to breed our garden carrot. The young taproots of this plant can be eaten in the spring.

FLOWER: 3"–5"   HEIGHT: 1'–3'   BLOOMS: May–Oct.

Diapensia
Diapensia lapponica

DIAPENSIA FAMILY. White, waxy, bell-shaped corolla flowers have five round spreading lobes and five yellow stamens. Flowers grow singly from short stalks. Leather-like narrow leaves grow in tight basal rosettes and form a spongy thick evergreen mat that enables this uncommon native flower to withstand severe wind and cold. Found at high altitude on barren ledges and sheltered beneath rocky ledges in the alpine areas of the White Mountains.

FLOWER: ½"   **HEIGHT:** 1"–3"   **BLOOMS:** June–July

Bunchberry

Cornus canadensis

DOGWOOD FAMILY. This seemingly simple flower is actually a cluster of small flowers surrounded by four white petal-like leaves (bracts). This low shrub has a woody rhizome and a whorl of deeply veined, shiny dark green oval leaves just beneath the flower head. This New Hampshire native has small, almost tasteless red berries that were used as a survival food in colonial times. Found in forests of all elevations and in the alpine zone.

FLOWER: 1"–2"   **HEIGHT:** 4"–6"   **BLOOMS:** June–Aug.

Turtle Head   *Chelone glabra*

FIGWORT FAMILY. Several white flowers, occasionally tinged with pink, appear in dense clusters surrounded by bracts atop smooth branching stems. Upper and lower petals form a closed two-lipped corolla that is shaped like a turtle's head. Opposite, lance-shaped finely toothed leaves bear a raised mid-rib. Native to New Hampshire, it is found in swamps, bogs, thickets and near streams.

FLOWER: 1"–1½"   **HEIGHT:** 1'–3'   **BLOOMS:** July–Sept.

133

Cow Wheat

Melampyrum lineare

FIGWORT FAMILY. Paired, tube-like white corolla flowers appear like snake heads on the upper stem of this native plant. The hood-shaped upper lip is bearded and the lower lip has three yellow-tipped lobes; the central lobe resembles a protruding tongue. Leaves are opposite, short-stalked and lance-shaped with smooth edges except for sword-shaped teeth at their base. This semi-parasitic plant forms dense colonies in dry open woodlands and near blueberry stands.

FLOWER: 1"–2"   **HEIGHT:** 8"–15"   **BLOOMS:** June–Aug.

Squirrel Corn   *Dicentra canadensis*

FUMITORY FAMILY. Small, two-lobed white flowers
hang upside down from leafless stalks above a bed of
dark-green, finely divided, feathery leaves. The root-
stalk has corn-like tubers, hence the common name
"squirrel corn." The plant contains toxic alkaloids poisonous to animals and it is therefore not actually eaten
by squirrels. This rare native leafy herb, considered
threatened in New Hampshire, is found in enriched
woodlands.

FLOWER: ³/₄"–1"   HEIGHT: 4"–10"   BLOOMS: April–May

Dutchman's Breeches   *Dicentra cucullaria*

FUMITORY FAMILY. Pantaloon-shaped, greenish-white flowers with yellow petal tips hang in linear clusters. Flowers grow on leafless stalks over a dark bed of finely divided compound leaves. Flowers are often seen with holes through their sides created by bees which cannot reach the nectar from the flower's opening. This native leafy herb is found in enriched woodlands. Its Parsley-like leaves are considered poisonous.

FLOWER: ³⁄₄"   **HEIGHT:** 4"–12"   **BLOOM:** April–May

Wild Sarsaparilla   *Aralia nudicaulis*

GINSENG FAMILY. Flowers are distinctively arranged in globe-shaped, two-inch diameter clusters atop leafless stalks. Each minute, greenish-white flower has five long stamens giving the globes a fuzzy appearance. The flower clusters are overshadowed by separate leaf stalks with pinnately compound leaves composed of five finely toothed leaflets. This native aromatic flower is common in upland forests. Native Americans used the plant to make a cough remedy. It was also used by colonists to make tea and as a flavoring for root beer.

FLOWER: 1/8"   HEIGHT: 12"–15"   BLOOMS: May–June

Dwarf Ginseng

Panax trifolius

GINSENG FAMILY: Terminal umbrella-shaped cluster of five-petalled, whitish-pink flowers with five protruding stamens. Fertilized flowers form several yellow berries. This herb has three compound leaves, composed of five lance-shaped toothed leaflets, which appear in a whorl at base of the flower stem. This is *not* the species noted for its healing qualities. This plant is found in moist woods.

FLOWER: 1/16"   **HEIGHT:** 4"–8"   **BLOOMS:** April–May

Leather-leaf   *Chamaedaphne calyculata*

HEATH FAMILY. Greenish-white, bell-shaped flowers with recurved petal tips hang in a terminal linear cluster. Flowers are found amid alternating oval leaves with finely toothed edges. The leaves' surface resembles leather and gives rise to this plant's folk name "Leather-leaf." This many-branched, low evergreen shrub is a native of New Hampshire and is found in bogs, in wetlands and at the edges of ponds.

FLOWER: ¼"   HEIGHT: 2'–4'   BLOOMS: April–May

Wintergreen

Gaultheria procumbens

HEATH FAMILY. Clusters of stalked, white, nodding, bell-shaped corolla flowers have five lobes which spread outward as the flower matures. This dwarf creeping evergreen shrub has short erect stems with alternating, pointed, toothed, oval leaves forming a canopy over the flowers. This plant's fragrant wintergreen leaves and red edible berries were used by Native Americans to make teas to treat the common cold. Native to New Hampshire's dry and moist shady acidic woodlands.

FLOWER: 1/4"–3/8" **HEIGHT:** 15" creeper **BLOOMS:** June–July

Labrador Tea   *Rhododendron groenlandicum*

HEATH FAMILY. Dense terminal clusters of white flowers with five petals and five to seven protruding stamens grow on this evergreen shrub. Fragrant, narrow,
short-stalked, shiny oval leaves with a hairy underside
alternate on hairy twigs. First discovered on the island
of Labrador, European colonists used its leaves to make
tea, hence the common name "Labrador Tea." This
New Hampshire native is found in bogs, woodlands
and on the rocky slopes of alpine areas of the White
Mountains.

FLOWER: ¹/₃"   HEIGHT: 1'–3'   BLOOMS: May–July

Hobblebush

Viburnum lantanoides

HONEYSUCKLE FAMILY. A fragrant native shrub with clusters of brilliant white five-petalled outer flowers surrounding smaller white inner flowers. Deep green, heart-shaped opposing leaves with finely toothed edges grow on woody stems. It is noted for blazing red-purple foliage in autumn. Found in cool woodlands, Hobblebush provides cover and food for wildlife. Branches bend and form loops near the ground, which catch the feet of hikers hence the name "hobble" bush.

FLOWER: 1"   **HEIGHT:** 3'–10'   **BLOOMS:** May–June

142

Highbush Cranberry
Viburnum opulus var. americanum

HONEYSUCKLE FAMILY. Flowers are arranged in flat-topped clusters composed of bright white, five-lobed outer flowers surrounding smaller greenish inner flowers. Leaves are opposite, palmately veined and three-lobed, each lobe with a pointed tip. Native Americans used the berries as a food source and made a medicinal tea from the bark to ease menstrual cramps. This New Hampshire native shrub is found in moist soil near streams and woodlands.

FLOWER: 3" cluster   HEIGHT: 3'–10'   BLOOMS: June–July

Indian Pipe   *Monotropa uniflora*

INDIAN PIPE FAMILY. Waxy-white or pale pink translucent solitary nodding flowers with four to five petals have ten to twelve stamens and a pistil. At maturity
the flower becomes erect and the whole plant turns
black. Scale-like white leaves alternate up the fleshy
stem. This native plant is well-adapted to the forest
floor where sunlight is scarce because it obtains nourishment from decaying organic matter through a dense
fiber-like root system. Its leaves do not have the chlorophyll necessary for photosynthesis.

FLOWER: ½"–1"   HEIGHT: 3"–9"   BLOOMS: June–Sept.

Canada Mayflower *Maianthemum canadense*

LILY FAMILY. A forest herb with tiny white flowers growing in a terminal cluster. Each flower has two petal-like sepals, two petals, and four stamens. Fruit is a white berry that turns red in the fall. Two to three alternating shiny heart-shaped leaves clasp a smooth stem below the flower cluster. This native member of the lily family forms colonies in moist shady woodlands and sheltered alpine areas. Sometimes called "false lily of the valley" it is a valuable food source for grouse and small mammals.

FLOWER: ⅛"   HEIGHT: 2"–6"   BLOOMS: May–June

False Solomon's Seal

Maianthemum racemosum

LILY FAMILY. Minute white flowers have three petals, three sepals and six stamens. Flowers are arranged in three- to six-inch long often drooping branched terminal clusters. Oval leaves, with pointed tips and prominent parallel veins, alternate along a zigzag stem. This plant's thick rhizomatous roots were eaten by Native Americans after they were soaked in lye and parboiled to make them edible. This New Hampshire native herb is found in woods, in clearings and on roadsides.

FLOWER: ⅛"   **HEIGHT:** 2'–3'   **BLOOMS:** May–July

Large White Trillium   *Trillium grandiflorum*

LILY FAMILY. A pleasant scent and large white petals
that turn pink as the flower ages make this flower a
favorite of wildflower gardeners. A single flower, with
six bright yellow stamens and prominent bean-shaped
anthers, sits on an erect stalk over a whorl of three
large diamond-shaped leaves. Roots were chewed by
Native Americans to relieve heart arrhythmia and the
pains of childbirth. This New Hampshire native is
found in rich woods and at the shaded edges of fields
and streams.

FLOWER: 2"–4"   HEIGHT: 12"–16"   BLOOMS: April–June

Snowy Trillium

Trillium simile

LILY FAMILY. This "garden escapee" is a native of the Smoky Mountains where it is known as the Sweet Wake-robin because of its pleasant scent. The flower has a triangular arrangement of light yellow stamens and short white to pinkish-white petals on a nodding stalk that protrudes above a whorl of three large leaves. Although it is not generally considered naturalized, its presence in the White Mountains is probably the result of its popularity within the wildflower gardening community in recent decades.

FLOWER: 1"–2"   **HEIGHT:** 8"–14"   **BLOOMS:** April–July

Painted Trillium   *Trillium undulatum*

LILY FAMILY. This New Hampshire native has three wavy-edged white petals with crimson veins, three long-pointed sepals, and six pink tipped stamens. Three large pointed oval leaves form a whorl at the base of the flower's stalk. This flower has an unattractive smell to most creatures except carrion flies. Animals and birds help spread this plant when its seeds survive their digestion. Its delicate root system is harmed by picking its flowers. Forms colonies in moist deep woods.

FLOWER: 2"–2½"   HEIGHT: 8"–20"   BLOOMS: April–June

Lily of the Valley   *Convallaria majalis*

Lily of the Valley family. Linear terminal clusters of fragrant nodding globe-shaped flowers with downward pointing recurved petals are found on a curved flower stalk. Two to three long, parallel-veined pointed leaves surround the stem. This naturalized European garden escapee is now occasionally found in colonies in pine and hardwood forests and at the edges of fields. Its red berries and roots are considered poisonous.

Flower: 1/3"   **Height:** 10"   **Blooms:** May–June

Starry False Solomon's Seal
Maianthemum stellatum

LILY OF THE VALLEY FAMILY. Several small bright white flowers alternate in an unbranched cluster atop a slender solitary stem. Flowers have six narrow, petal-like segments and six curving stamens. This creeping rhizomatous herb has black-striped berries. Bluish-green, lance-shaped clasping leaves alternate on a slightly zig-zag stalk. This New Hampshire native flower is found in sandy woods, well-drained thickets and near swamps.

FLOWER: ³/₈"   **HEIGHT:** 8"–20"   **BLOOMS:** May–June

Northern Bedstraw

Galium boreale

MADDER FAMILY. This tall weak-stemmed native herb overtakes and reclines on surrounding vegetation. Compact branches have terminal clusters with white, sharply tipped, four-petalled flowers and four protruding stamens. The sepals are absent. Leaves are lance-shaped to linear. Found growing in rocky wet soil near stream-banks and in thickets.

FLOWER: ¼"   **HEIGHT:** 8"–36"   **BLOOMS:** June–Aug.

Wild Madder

Galium mollugo

MADDER FAMILY. This plant has closely spaced clusters of minute four-petalled flowers with prominent stamens. Clusters arranged in branching groups on stems above whorls of six to eight smooth, lance-shaped leaves. Naturalized from Europe, this flower is now commonly found in open fields, meadows and pastures.

FLOWER: 1/4"   **HEIGHT:** 1'–3'   **BLOOMS:** June–Aug.

153

Alpine Bluet

Houstonia caerulea

MADDER FAMILY. This sweet-scented alpine form of Bluet has snowy white, delicate funnel-shaped four-petalled flowers with bright yellowish gold centers. Stamens are varied in length. Leaves are tiny, opposite and arranged in a basal rosette near the ground. This flower forms beautiful carpets of white and gold as it blooms in its habitat: sheltered alpine areas of the White Mountains.

FLOWER: ½"   **HEIGHT:** 2"–4"   **BLOOMS:** June–July

Partridge-berry
Mitchella repens

MADDER FAMILY. Fragrant funnel-shaped white flowers have four fuzzy lobes. They appear in pairs joined at the base by their ovaries which form twin red berries. Opposing, shiny green, round leaves with white veins appear on creeping, branched stems creating a dense mat on the forest floor. This native evergreen plant, found in acidic woodlands, was used medicinally by Native American women to ease childbirth.

FLOWER: 1/2"–5/8"   **HEIGHT:** 4"–12"   **BLOOMS:** June–July

155

Garlic Mustard
Alliaria petiolata

MUSTARD FAMILY. Terminal clusters of small, white flowers with four petals, four sepals and six stamens appear on short branching stalks on a thick erect central stem. Triangular, deeply toothed, stalked leaves are found beneath the flower cluster. This naturalized European herb is considered an invasive plant in the White Mountains. Its leaves have a garlic-like odor when crushed and were used by colonists as a substitute for garlic flavoring.

FLOWER: ¼"   HEIGHT: 1"–3"   BLOOMS: April–June

Broad-leafed Toothwort *Cardamine diphylla*

Mustard family. This plant has several small, stalked, white flowers in a loose terminal cluster on an unbranched stem. Flowers have four petals, four sepals and six erect stamens. Two compound leaves, each composed of three bluntly toothed oval leaflets, appear opposite each other near the middle of the stem. This native flower is found in wet areas of woodlands, in bogs and in swamps. Flowers turn pink with age and the edible roots taste like horseradish.

Flower: ⁵⁄₈"   **Height:** 1'   **Blooms:** April–May

White-fringed Orchid
Platanthera blephariglottis

ORCHID FAMILY. China-white flowers with a prominent, fringed, lip petal are found in a terminal cluster on the top third of an erect stem. Three egg-shaped sepals and a long curved spur complete this showy native orchid flower. Two long, narrow, lance-shaped basal leaves and much smaller bract-like upper leaves appear on the stem. This somewhat rare exquisite flower is found in sphagnum moss bogs, seeps and along pondsides and is on the "state watch" list.

FLOWER: 1¹/₂"   **HEIGHT:** 1'–2'   **BLOOMS:** July–Aug.

Bog White Orchis   *Platanthera dilatata*

ORCHID FAMILY. Vertical clusters of small "winged" flowers spiral up a vertical stem. Flowers are subtended by narrow, lance-shaped leaves which cling to the stem. Flower has a classic orchid shape: a prominent lower lip with two wing-like slightly recurved sepals on either side. The remaining petals and sepals form a hood above the lip. This striking native orchid is found in wet cool meadows and forests up through the alpine elevations.

FLOWER: 1" wide   **HEIGHT:** 1'–2'   **BLOOMS:** June–July

159

Nodding Ladies Tresses   *Spiranthes cernua*

ORCHID FAMILY. The White Mountain's most common fall orchid, it is often seen growing in large stands. Vertical spirals of 30 or more small white hooded flowers appear at the top of tall stems. White sepals and petals form a tube with a small wavy lip. Several narrow green leaves grow near the base of the stem with small leaves farther up. Occasionally found in moist fields, open seeps and along country roads.

FLOWER: ¹/₃"   HEIGHT: 15"–20"   BLOOMS: Aug.–Oct.

Yellow Nodding Ladies Tresses
Spiranthes ochroleuca

ORCHID FAMILY. Twenty to sixty small, white to yellow-tinged flowers, in three rows, spiral up a vertical stem. The flower's upper lip is shaped like a hood over the downward curving fringed lower lip petal. Lateral sepals are spike-like and point forward along the side. Upper leaves clasp the stem in a spiral intertwined with the flowers. Long narrow basal leaves grow up the stem. This uncommon late blooming native orchid is found in dry, partly shaded woodlands and at woodland edges.

FLOWER: 2/5"   HEIGHT: 6"–15"   BLOOMS: Sept.–Oct.

Hooded Ladies Tresses
Spiranthes romanzoffiana

ORCHID FAMILY. Twenty to sixty small white flowers, in three rows, spiral up a vertical stem. The upper lip is formed from one sepal and two petals and is shaped like a hood over the downward-curving, fringed lower lip petal. Lateral sepals are spike-like and point forward along the side. Small upper leaves clasp the stem and three to six long narrow basal leaves grow along the stem. This uncommon native orchid is found in open or partly shaded areas of bogs, in seeps or at the edges of ponds.

FLOWER: ½"   **HEIGHT:** 6"–20"   **BLOOMS:** July–Sept.

Rabbit's-foot Clover   *Trifolium arvense*

PEA/BEAN FAMILY. The flowerhead is arranged in distinctive cylindrical clusters of tiny pink-gray flowers. Sepals have long fine hairs which give the cluster the appearance of fine fur, like a "rabbit's foot." Leaves, finely haired, are divided into three narrow leaflets. This naturalized European annual is often found in stands growing in fields, meadows and along roads.

FLOWER: 3/4" clusters **HEIGHT:** 6"–18" **BLOOMS:** June–Aug.

White Clover

Trifolium repens

PEA/BEAN FAMILY. Many minute white flowers appear in a round terminal cluster that is tinged at the base with pink. Often called "shamrocks," three palmately compound oval leaves appear on separate stalks. Found in fields, meadows and lawns, this naturalized European flower's presence helps enrich the soil with nitrogen. This is an important plant for honey bees because its nectar is plentiful and it is a valuable food source for birds, mammals and livestock.

FLOWER: ³/₄"–1"   **HEIGHT:** 4"–10"   **BLOOMS:** May–Sept.

Mouse Ear Chickweed

Cerastium fontanum ssp. vulgare

PINK FAMILY. Small white flowers have five petals cleft half way down their length. Green sepals are wide and nearly as long as the petals. Flowers often appear in branched clusters on a stalks above hairy oval leaves. This naturalized European herb is now an important animal food source. It spreads through seeds that survive the digestive process of animals.

FLOWER: 1/2"–3/4"   HEIGHT: 6"–18"   BLOOMS: May–Aug.

Glabrous Sandwort · *Minuartia glabra*

PINK FAMILY. This close relative of the mountain sandwort is found in moss-covered rocky areas, usually
below 1000 meters. Considered endangered in New
Hampshire, this native flower is similar in appearance
to the mountain sandwort, both having five notched
white petals. Unlike the mountain sandwort, its sepals
are much shorter than the petals and its leaves do not
form large mats. The flowers appear on delicate
branching stems over small tufts of narrow leaves.

FLOWER: ½"   **HEIGHT:** 2"–5"   **BLOOMS:** May–Aug.

Mountain Sandwort *Minuartia groenlandica*

PINK FAMILY. White flowers with five notched petals
sit atop branching stalks with small pin-like green
leaves. Known in the White Mountains as "Mountain
Daisy" because its blooms form fields of white along
trails in alpine soils. The leaves of this native flower
form tufted mats near mossy areas of granite slabs, in
cracks and near sandy alpine areas. Usually growing
on summits above 1000 meters, this is a "state watch"
species in New Hampshire.

FLOWER: ½"   HEIGHT: 2"–5"   BLOOMS: June–Aug.

White Campion *Silene latifolia*

PINK FAMILY. Flowers have white to pinkish-white, deeply notched petals on a bladder-shaped calyx. Flowers are arranged in loose terminal clusters. Leaves are opposite and lance-shaped. Separate male and female plants help insure cross-pollination. Introduced from Europe, it is now common in meadows, fields and along roads.

FLOWER: 1"   **HEIGHT:** 1'–3'   **BLOOMS:** July–Oct.

Bladder Campion

Silene vulgaris

PINK FAMILY. Flower has five deeply notched curved petals and protruding stamens that emerge from a navel-like depression at the end of a large, deeply veined bladder-shaped calyx. Generally plants are either male or female but some are bisexual. Long, thin, lance-like leaves often clasp the stem. This European immigrant is now common in fields, meadows and along roads.

FLOWER: 1"   **HEIGHT:** 8"–30"   **BLOOMS:** April–Aug.

Lesser Stitchwort   *Stellaria graminea*

PINK FAMILY. Small white flowers have five deeply divided petals appearing like ten. The flower sits atop a very slender stalk over small, narrowly lance-shaped leaves that form a grass-like mat below. In colonial times a tea made from the plant was thought to be a cure-all. Introduced from Europe, it is found in fields and meadows.

FLOWER: ¹/₂"   **HEIGHT:** 10"–20"   **BLOOMS:** May–Sept.

Bloodroot *Sanguinaria canadensis*

POPPY FAMILY. This short-lived early spring flower sits on a long stem encircled by a single, deeply scalloped palm-shaped leaf with irregular edges. Brilliant white oval petals surround numerous golden stamens. The red sap of this native flower was used by Native Americans to make a dye. Found in deep woodlands and along streams, it opens only in sunlight, and is a "state watch" species in New Hampshire.

FLOWER: 1"–1½" **HEIGHT:** 5"–10" **BLOOMS:** March–May

Starflower   *Trientalis borealis*

PRIMROSE FAMILY. Delicate flowers have five to nine pointed petals around a yellow center with protruding yellow-tipped stamens. Each plant usually bears one or two flowers on long thin stalks over a single whorl of shiny lance-shaped leaves with tapered points. It is the only member of the primrose family which is found above timberline. This native plant is also seen in moist woods and bogs.

FLOWER: ½"–⅔"   **HEIGHT:** 3"–9"   **BLOOMS:** May–July

Woodland Strawberry   *Fragaria vesca*

ROSE FAMILY. This close relative of the common strawberry has smaller, more rounded petals. Flowers are found in clusters on stalks which usually rise above leaves. The leaves are composed of three, finely toothed oval leaflets. The fruit is similar to common strawberry but the seeds sit on the surface of the small reddish fruit. A favorite food source of birds and other animals, this native creeper is found in open woods and fields.

FLOWER: ½"   HEIGHT: 3"–6"   BLOOMS: April–June

Common Strawberry   *Fragaria virginiana*

ROSE FAMILY. Clusters made of small white flowers with five petals and five shorter sepals surround a yellow center with many stamens. Compound leaves composed of three large-toothed oval leaflets appear on separate finely haired stalks and usually grow slightly taller than the flowers. This native creeper produces a sweet red fruit with seeds indented into the fruit's surface. A tea made from this plant's vitamin C rich leaves helped save American revolutionary forces from the dreaded disease scurvy. Found in woods and fields.

FLOWER: 1/2"   **HEIGHT:** 3"–6"   **BLOOMS:** April–June

Choke-cherry
Prunus virginiana

ROSE FAMILY. Dozens of small white flowers, each with five petals, are arranged in distinctive cylinder-shaped terminal clusters. The leaves are simple, oval, alternate, and finely toothed. Its small red fruit has a bitter taste due to the presence of hydrocyanic acid, hence the common name "choke cherry." The fruit, bark, and roots were widely used by Native Americans and European settlers as the base for medicinal teas, lozenges and skin treatments. This native shrub is found in fields, thickets and at woodland edges.

FLOWER: ½"   **HEIGHT:** 6'–20'   **BLOOMS:** May–June

Common Blackberry   *Rubus allegheniensis*

ROSE FAMILY. Flower clusters are composed of white five-petaled flowers with five sepals and numerous stamens. Leaves are palmately compound with three to five toothed leaflets. Stems of this native bramble are woody and thorny. Fruit is a sweet, oval, edible blackberry. This plant forms thickets in old fields, clearings and along country roads. Berries are a food source for birds and woodland mammals.

FLOWER: 1"   HEIGHT: 3'–8'   BLOOMS: May–July

Swamp Dewberry
Rubus hispidus

ROSE FAMILY. Flowers have five small, round, short-stemmed petals and numerous stamens. Flowers grow in terminal clusters on bristly branches surrounded by finely toothed oval leaves. This native creeper sends out long runners that bear new flowering branches in the second year. It is found in acidic swamps, wet open woods and at the edges of ponds and streams.

FLOWER: ½"–¾"   HEIGHT: 6"–12"   BLOOMS: June–Aug.

Wild Red Raspberry

Rubus idaeus

Rose family. White flowers have five widely spaced narrow oval petals, five sepals and numerous stamens. Flowers appear singly or in clusters growing at the tip of this native bramble's branches. The pinnately compound leaves are composed of three to seven sharply toothed leaflets and grow on reddish thorny stems. Fruit is a sweet edible red berry. Found in old fields, near woodlands, and along country roads, this native red raspberry is a favorite food of wild birds.

Flower: ½"   **Height:** 2'–5'   **Blooms:** May–June

Dwarf Raspberry   *Rubus pubescens*

ROSE FAMILY. This native raspberry creeps along the
ground on a non-woody stem. Small white flowers
have five narrow petals, five small pointed sepals and
numerous stamens. Flowers grow singly or in small clusters. Long stalked divided leaves (composed of three
sharply toothed pointed oval leaflets) alternate on
thornless branches. Fruit is a small edible red raspberry.
Found in New Hampshire's bogs, wet thickets, damp
woods and the alpine zone.

FLOWER: ½" **HEIGHT:** 2"–6" creeper **BLOOMS:** May–June

Three-toothed Cinquefoil
Sibbaldiopsis tridentata

Rose family. White flowers with four to five rounded petals and many stamens grow in small terminal clusters on branching stems. Evergreen leaves are composed of three leaflets, each with three large tooth-like indents at their tip. The plant spreads through underground stems. Native to the White Mountains' exposed rocky alpine areas, subalpine rocky summits and sandy shorelines of high-elevation ponds.

Flower: ¹/₄"–¹/₂" **Height:** 1"–12" **Blooms:** July–Sept.

Meadow Sweet   *Spiraea alba var. latifolia*

ROSE FAMILY. Dense terminal clusters are composed of minute five-petalled white to pinkish-white flowers with stamens that protrude beyond small round petals. Flower clusters are longer than wide and narrow at the tip. Broadly oval leaves have pointed tips and coarse teeth. This native New Hampshire shrub is found in fields and meadows. It is an important food source for deer.

FLOWER: ¹⁄₆"–¹⁄₄"   HEIGHT: 6"–6'   BLOOMS: June–Aug.

Two-leafed Miterwort　　　*Mitella diphylla*

Saxifrage family: Slender vertical clusters of minute, white, cup-shaped flowers alternate on a single hairy stem. Flowers have delicate, elaborately fringed petals, ten stamens and one pistil. Upper leaves are maple-like, opposite and short stalked. Lower leaves are similar but have long stalks. This native plant can be seen alone or in colonies in rich moist woods and near seeps. Flowers bloom before woodland trees fully leaf out.

Flower: ⅛"　　　**Height:** 8"–18"　　　**Blooms:** April–June

Early Saxifrage

Saxifraga virginiensis

SAXIFRAGE FAMILY. Branching clusters of fragrant white flowers sit atop the leafless stalks of this early blooming rhizomatous plant. Small flowers with five petals, two pistils and one yellow stamen spread out from a sticky hairy stem. Toothed oval leaves with a purplish underside form a rosette at the base of the plant. This native flower is found on moist to dry rock ledges, in gorges and on cliffs. Young leaves are edible and were cooked as greens by colonists.

FLOWER: ¼"   **HEIGHT:** 4"–16"   **BLOOMS:** April–June

Foam Flower

Tiarella cordifolia

SAXIFRAGE FAMILY. Small, white, feathery flowers are arranged in elongated vertical terminal clusters on a leafless stalk. Five narrow petals, five narrow sepals and ten protruding stamens give this flower the fuzzy appearance of sea foam when it is viewed from a distance. Grows in colonies through underground rhizomes. Its basal maple-like leaves are found on stalks separate from those of the flowers. This New Hampshire native flower is an important autumn food source for wild birds.

FLOWER: ¼" **HEIGHT:** 6"–12" **BLOOMS:** May–June

Cotton Grass
Eriophorum vaginatum

SEDGE FAMILY. Bright white tufts of cotton-like hairs arranged in a terminal cluster resemble a rabbit's tail. The minute flowers are arranged in tufts of bristly hairs with sepals and petals being absent. A grass-shaped sheath surrounds the base of the triangular erect stem. This native sedge spreads through a creeping underground rhizome. Cotton Grass is found from cold peat bogs of lowland forests to wetlands in the alpine zone.

FLOWER: 1"–1½" HEIGHT: 6"–12" BLOOMS: May–July

Round-leaved Sundew *Drosera rotundifolia*

SUNDEW FAMILY. Small, five-petalled white flowers on leafless stalks emerge from a basal rosette of reddish leaves. The leaves are covered with gland-tipped hairs whose secretion of sticky fluid traps insects, which are then digested by enzymes. This flower's ability to extract nutrition from insects helps it survive in nutrient-poor bogs and marshes.

FLOWER: ¼"   **HEIGHT:** 4"–9"   **BLOOMS:** June–Aug.

Red-stemmed Violet

Viola blanda

VIOLET FAMILY. This is a small fragrant "stemless" (flower and leaves on separate stalks) violet with a reddish tinge to its flower stalk and distinctive floppy or twisted upper petals. The whole plant is generally hairless except for sparse hairs beneath the lower leaves. Flower head usually rises above the surrounding heart-shaped leaves. This native New Hampshire violet is found in rich moist woods, in ravines and near stands of evergreens.

FLOWER: ¹/₄"–¹/₂" **HEIGHT:** 2"–4" **BLOOMS:** April–May

Canadian Violet

Viola canadensis

VIOLET FAMILY. This is a "stemmed" (flowers and leaves on the same central stem) white violet with a yellow eyespot near the center of the flower. Lateral petals have small yellow beards. The lower three petals have brown-purple veins. The backs and tips of all petals are tinged with purple. Leaves are heart-shaped, bluntly toothed and short-stalked. Minute hairs grow on stems, stalks, and on small, smooth-edged stipules. This native violet is found in rich, moist, deciduous woods and is "state watch" in New Hampshire.

FLOWER: ½"– ⅔"   **HEIGHT:** 6"–12"   **BLOOMS:** April–May

Alpine Marsh Violet   *Viola palustris*

VIOLET FAMILY. This small white (sometimes pale lavender) "stemless" violet has beards on its lateral petals, dark veins on its lower petal, and its flower hangs at leaf level from its own stalk. A short rounded spur protrudes from the back of the flower. Wide, heart-shaped, shallowly toothed leaves have a nearly closed notch (sinus) at their base. This native violet, common in sub-arctic areas to our north, is considered endangered in New Hampshire. It is found in wet, protected alpine areas and near sub-alpine streams and ravines.

FLOWER: ½"   **HEIGHT:** 2"–4"   **BLOOMS:** May–July

Arrowhead

Sagittaria latifolia

WATER-PLANTAIN FAMILY. White flowers appear in whorls of three on tall thin stalks that rise from the water. Flowers have three petals, three sepals and seven to ten yellow stamens. Large arrow-shaped basal leaves vary from narrow to wide. This native aquatic plant is found in the muddy quiet waters of bogs and marshes. Also known as "duck potatoes," the edible starchy underwater tubers were harvested by Native Americans. This plant is a valuable food source for muskrats and wood ducks.

FLOWER: ⁵/₈"   **HEIGHT:** 1'–4'   **BLOOMS:** July–Sept.

Small Pussy Willow

Salix humilis

WILLOW FAMILY. Known in New Hampshire as one of the first signs of spring, the flowers of this native shrub are a favorite of children because the flowers feel like a kitten's soft fur. Flowers bloom in small alternate clusters before the appearance of leaves. Male plants have bright yellow flower clusters and female plants white-gray clusters. This shrub is found in fields, thickets, swamps and along streams.

FLOWER: 1"–2"   **HEIGHT:** 3'–6'   **BLOOMS:** March–May

Shinleaf
Pyrola elliptica

HEATH FAMILY. Fragrant, nodding, waxy-white five-petalled flowers grow in loose vertical clusters. Flowers have ten stamens, one pistil and one long upward curling style. Broadly oblong, stalked evergreen leaves grow from the base of the plant around an erect reddish stem. Native Americans used this plant's crushed leaves to dress bruises and wounds. This native rhizomatous herb is found in moist to dry woodlands.

FLOWER: 1/2"–3/4" **HEIGHT:** 5"–10" **BLOOMS:** June–Aug.

Joe Pye Weed   *Eupatoriadelphus maculatus*

ASTER FAMILY. Many tiny purple-pink, five-lobed tube flowers appear in branched terminal clusters on a tall stem that is usually colored purple or has purple spots. Hair-like styles protrude from flower tubes giving a fuzzy appearance. Lance-shaped toothed leaves grow in whorls of four to five. This native flower is found in wet meadows, fields, thickets and along shores of ponds and streams. Named after Joe Pye, an Algonquin Native American healer, who is said to have cured typhoid fever using this plant.

FLOWER: 4–6" cluster **HEIGHT:** 3'–6' **BLOOMS:** July–Sept.

Cardinal Flower   *Lobelia cardinalis*

BELLFLOWER FAMILY. Bright red flowers, said to resemble a churchman's official hat, alternate on the upper portion of stout vertical stems. A five-sided calyx appears beneath a brilliant red five-lobed corolla. The three bottom lobes hang down and the other two lobes appear like wings on the side. The stamens form a vertical red tube around the style and this structure is topped off with a white-tipped stigma. Leaves are lance-shaped and toothed. This appealing native Lobelia is becoming less common due to overpicking.

FLOWER: 1½"–2½"   HEIGHT: 2'–5'   BLOOMS: July–Sept.

Wild Ginger

Asarum canadense

BIRTHWORT FAMILY. A single cup-shaped flower, often covered with forest litter, rests on or near the ground between two large oval leaves. Each leaf is on its own very hairy stem. The face of the flower has three pointed reddish-brown lobes. European colonists ground the root to use as a substitute for ginger. This native perennial herb grows in enriched forests and is "state watch" in New Hampshire.

FLOWER: 1–1½"   **HEIGHT:** 6"–12"   **BLOOMS:** April–May

Wild Columbine   *Aquilegia canadensis*

BUTTERCUP FAMILY. Bell-shaped nodding flowers with yellow centers hang on a delicate branched stem. Flower has five spur-topped red petals, five petal-like sepals and numerous stamens that extend below the petals. Alternate upper compound leaves are divided into three-lobed leaflets. Lower leaves are larger and long-stalked. This native rhizomatous herb is found in dry, rich woods, on shaded ledges, and in ravines. It is a favorite nectar source for the ruby-throated hummingbird.

FLOWER: 1"–2"   **HEIGHT:** 1'–2'   **BLOOMS:** April–June

Spreading Dogbane

Apocynum androsaemifolium

DOGBANE FAMILY. Small, nodding, pink bell-shaped flowers grow in terminal clusters on this fragrant native herb. Flowers have spreading lobes that are striped pink and white inside. Leaves are opposite, stalked, and oval with a hairy underside and smooth edges. A milky sap oozes from the stem when broken. It is found in moist fields, thickets and meadows and is known to be poisonous to humans and animals.

FLOWER: 3/8"   **HEIGHT:** 1'–4'   **BLOOMS:** June–Aug.

Pale Corydalis   *Corydalis sempervirens*

FUMITORY FAMILY. This delicate native biennial forms short clusters of pink and yellow flowers growing from thin, branched stems above bluish-green, pinnately-divided lobed leaflets. A distinctive pink spur growing upward from the petals identifies this flower. This native herb is found on rich humus mats near rocky outcrops.

FLOWER: ¼"–½"   **HEIGHT:** 5"–24"   **BLOOMS:** May–Sept.

Herb Robert

Geranium robertianum

Geranium family. One or more pink, five-petalled flowers grow on reddish branching hairy stems. Leaves are divided into three to five pinnately lobed leaflets. The end-most leaflets are lobed to their base and usually have a short stalk. This geranium is found in moist woodlands, near seeps and wet rocky slopes. Some experts consider local populations native, others believe local plants came from European stock.

Flower: ½" **Height:** 1'–2' **Blooms:** May–Oct.

Trailing Arbutus   *Epigaea repens*

Heath family. Small, pink five-lobed fragrant flowers are found in terminal clusters on hairy stems. Small oval evergreen leaves alternate on slender woody branches that "trail" along the forest floor. Also known as "Mayflower," this early blooming evergreen is often obscured by leaf litter on the forest floor. A New Hampshire native, it is found in sandy woods.

Flower: ½"   **Height:** 6"   **Blooms:** April–May

Sheep Laurel   *Kalmia angustifolia*

HEATH FAMILY. Pentagon-shaped, shallowly lobed pink
flowers appear in lateral clusters below whorls of leaves.
Flowers have ten stamens whose anthers fit into pockets on the flower's lobes. Smooth oval leaves with a
prominent central vein appear in whorls of three. This
native evergreen shrub is found in moist acidic soils
in bogs and wet woodlands. This plant gained the folk
name "sheep kill" because it is poisonous to livestock.

FLOWER: ½"   HEIGHT: 2'–3'   BLOOMS: May–July

Bog Laurel

Kalmia polifolia

HEATH FAMILY. This branched evergreen shrub produces terminal clusters of pink, pentagon-shaped five-petalled flowers each with ten stamens. Anthers are hidden in pockets and protrude when touched, releasing pollen. Opposite, shiny, oblong leaves with rolled edges grow on this shrub's slender twigs. This native plant, noted as poisonous to livestock, grows in bogs up through the alpine zone.

FLOWER: ³⁄₈"–¹⁄₂"   **HEIGHT:** 1'–3'   **BLOOMS:** May–Aug.

Alpine Azalea   *Loiseleuria procumbens*

HEATH FAMILY. This plant has small clusters of pink to white bell-shaped flowers with five spreading petals. This showy dwarf creeping evergreen shrub forms dense mats in the rocky exposed areas of the alpine zone. Leaves are shiny and leather-like, narrowly oblong, opposite and short-stalked. This beautiful native flower, considered threatened in New Hampshire, creates a garden-like feeling where it grows on mountain summits.

FLOWER: ¼"   HEIGHT: 4" creeper   BLOOMS: June–Aug.

Mountain Heath

Phyllodoce caerulea

HEATH FAMILY. This plant has terminal clusters of rose to lavender nodding bell-shaped flowers. Each flower has a five-lobed corolla, five sepals and ten stamens. This native evergreen has slender twigs and grows near the ground, branching out and forming mats. Leaves are alternate, tiny, narrow and needle-like. This species, common in the Arctic, is considered threatened in New Hampshire. It is found in sheltered rocky alpine areas of the White Mountains.

FLOWER: ¹/₃"   **HEIGHT:** 4"–6"   **BLOOMS:** June–July

Rhodora
Rhododendron canadense

HEATH FAMILY. Lavender-pink flowers with upper and lower lips grow in terminal clusters on this native deciduous shrub. The upper lip is three-lobed with three ridges. The lower lip is divided into two tube-like segments with ten long protruding stamens. Flowers bloom before or just as leaves emerge. Alternate long to oblong grayish leaves have a hairy underside and rolled edges. Found in bogs, wooded swamps and at high elevations on rocky mountain ridges.

FLOWER: ³⁄₄"–1¹⁄₂"   **HEIGHT:** 1'–3'   **BLOOMS:** May–July

Low Bush Blueberry   *Vaccinium angustifolium*

HEATH FAMILY. Clusters of small bell-shaped flowers, each with five recurved pointed tips, bloom at the end of low bushy branches. Leaves are simple, alternate, oval to lance-shaped with finely toothed, red-tinged edges. Seen in diverse areas from the rocky soil of alpine regions to low moist woodlands. The fruit of this native shrub is a small blue berry with a sweet taste that is a favorite ingredient of baked goods and a favorite food of the bear as well.

FLOWER: 3/16"   HEIGHT: 4'–20'   BLOOMS: May–June

Small Cranberry
Vaccinium oxycoccos

HEATH FAMILY. Nodding, pink, four-lobed corolla flowers on red stalks have eight protruding stamens and a pistil. Small, alternate, leather-like oblong leaves grow on vertical branches. Creeping stems can form dense stands. Red edible cranberries mature in the fall and are a favorite food source of wildlife. This small native evergreen is found in acidic lowland areas and alpine bogs.

FLOWER: ¹⁄₄" **HEIGHT:** 4"–5" **BLOOMS:** June–July

Alpine Bilberry   *Vaccinium uliginosum*

Heath family. Bell-shaped, nodding, white to pink corolla flowers have four to five pointed recurved lobes. Flowers grow singly or in clusters on short stalks from the leaf axils. Round leathery toothless leaves alternate on this plant's reddish stem. The underside of the leaves are finely veined and pale. Fruit is an edible blue to black berry. This native bilberry is found in the open rocky or sandy areas of the alpine zone and is "state watch" in New Hampshire.

Flower: ¼"   **Height:** 6"–12"   **Blooms:** June–July

Mountain Cranberry   *Vaccinium vitis-idaea*

HEATH FAMILY. Terminal clusters of pink, nodding bell-shaped flowers grow on the upright branches of this low, creeping, evergreen shrub. Flowers have a four-lobed corolla with eight stamens. Leaves are alternate, shiny and oval with black dots on their underside. This native "cranberry" is found in rocky areas of the alpine zone and in lower elevation peat bogs and wet woodland areas. The bitter dark red berries have been used as a substitute for cranberries.

FLOWER: ¼"   HEIGHT: 3"–8"   BLOOMS: June–July

Twin Flower
Linnaea borealis

HONEYSUCKLE FAMILY. This plant has nodding, paired, fragrant pink and white bell-shaped, lobed corolla flowers with hairs inside. Rounded toothed leaves grow opposite along hairy, trailing, short branches. This native evergreen creeper is found in the cool woods and bogs of evergreen forests. A favorite food source for white tailed deer and Ruffed Grouse.

FLOWER: ½" **HEIGHT:** 3"–6" creeper **BLOOMS:** June–Aug.

Rose Twisted Stalk   *Streptopus lanceolatus*

LILY FAMILY. Pink to purple, nodding, bell-shaped flowers grow on short bent or curved stalks. Tip of flower is divided into six segments which curl backwards. Flower stalks hang below the base of long, lance-shaped, parallel-veined slightly clasping leaves, which alternate up a zigzag stem. This native flower is found in rich moist woods, thickets and clearings up to alpine elevations. Its round red berry is eaten by woodland birds and mammals.

FLOWER: ³⁄₈"   **HEIGHT:** 1'–3'   **BLOOMS:** April–July

Wake Robin
Trillium erectum

LILY FAMILY. This early spring flower has three crimson petals surrounded by three pointed but shorter green sepals on a nodding stalk over a whorl of three diamond-shaped leaves. Although beautiful, this flower has a pungent odor which attracts carrion flies for pollination. Its disagreeable scent has earned it the common name "Stinking Benjamin." This native flower is commonly found in colonies in moist rich woodlands and in shaded areas.

FLOWER: 3"–5"   **HEIGHT:** 6"–16"   **BLOOMS:** April–June

Sweet Beth
Trillium vaseyi

LILY FAMILY. This purple trillium is similar to the Wake Robin. Sweet Beth's flower has broader shorter petals and sepals, and sits nearly on top of its three oval leaves which appear in a whorl beneath the flower. This trillium has a soft sweet scent in contrast to the common Wake Robin, hence the name "Sweet Beth," sister to "Stinking Benjamin." This trillium, thought to be introduced by wildflower gardeners, is found in rich moist forest areas, often near its ill-scented relative.

FLOWER: 2"–5"   **HEIGHT:** 8"–16"   **BLOOMS:** April–June

Musk Mallow

Malva moschata

Mallow family. Pink to white five-petalled flowers appear in terminal clusters on slightly hairy stems. Prominent irregular notches on petals distinguish this species. Thin alternate leaves are palmately divided into three deeply-lobed sections. Some consider this naturalized European species to be potentially invasive because it may flourish in fields and pastures where it may rise above tall grasses.

Flower: 2"   **Height:** 2'   **Blooms:** June–Sept.

Milkweed

Asclepias syriaca

MILKWEED FAMILY. Many fragrant rose to beige colored flowers with five petals and a central, horned hood appear in round two-inch clusters. Leaves are opposite, waxy, oblong to oval, and with a soft underside. Plant oozes a milky sap when cut. Large, bumpy, wedge-shaped seed pods contain fluffy-haired seeds. The seeds were once used as stuffing for life jackets. Milkweed seeds are spread by the wind in late summer when seed pods open. This native flower is a host for the monarch butterfly larvae. Found in fields and along roads.

FLOWER: ½"   **HEIGHT:** 2'–6'   **BLOOMS:** June–Aug.

Wild Bergamot *Monarda fistulosa*

Mint family. Fragrant pink or lavender tube-shaped florets appear in clusters atop a square stem. Pale green opposite lance-shaped leaves are coarse-toothed and contain an aromatic oil. This naturalized mint grows in limestone enriched dry soil in woods, fields and thickets. Colonists used its leaves to make mint tea and its oil to soothe chest pains.

Flower: 1" **Height:** 2'–4' **Blooms:** June–Sept.

Cutleaf Toothwort *Cardamine concatenata*

Mustard family. Cross-shaped, delicate four-petalled flowers turn from white to pink as they age. Flowers sit in terminal clusters on a smooth unbranched stem. Leaves, composed of three to five slender coarse-toothed leaflets, appear in whorls of three. This native flower, considered endangered in New Hampshire, is found in rich moist woods and is a favorite nectar flower of bees. The name "toothwort" refers to tooth shaped growths on roots, which were ground and used by colonists as a substitute for horseradish.

Flower: ³/₄"   **Height:** 8"–15"   **Blooms:** April–May

Grass Pink

Calopogon tuberosus

ORCHID FAMILY. This "upside down" orchid has its lip petal on top. Pink petals and sepals resemble showy nectar flowers. When bees land on the lip petal looking for nectar in its yellow center, the lip collapses and the insects are covered with the orchid's pollen. Three or more flowers appear above one to two thin lance-shaped basal leaves. This native orchid is found in bogs, moist meadows and marshes.

FLOWER: 1"–2"   **HEIGHT:** 1'–3'   **BLOOMS:** June–July

Pink Lady's Slipper   *Cypripedium acaule*

ORCHID FAMILY. A distinctive pink, veined lower petal forms a balloon-like lip said to resemble a "lady's slipper." Two greenish-brown upper petals and three spreading pointed sepals extend over the lip petal. A pair of shiny, ribbed basal leaves with hairy undersides occur at the base of a leafless stalk. Found in dry sandy woods, on shaded humus covered rocks, and at high elevations. This showy large native orchid, often seen in colonies, rarely survives transplantation.

FLOWER: 2½"   **HEIGHT:** 6"–15"   **BLOOMS:** April–June

Rose Pogonia   *Pogonia ophioglossoides*

ORCHID FAMILY. A fragrant pink flower, usually solitary, has three petals and three petal-like, lance-shaped pink sepals. The bottom petal is ornately fringed with a bearded yellow center. The side petals and the sepals shield a long thin ovary. A solitary lance- to oval-shaped leaf is seen clasping the stem at about half the height of the flower. This showy native pogonia is found in sunny areas of open bogs, on river banks and in moist meadows.

FLOWER: 1¼"–1½"   **HEIGHT:** 8"–14"   **BLOOMS:** June–July

Crown-Vetch

Coronilla varia

PEA/BEAN FAMILY. Clusters of bi-colored pink and white flowers grow on a long erect stalk. Alternate pinnately-compound leaves grow on sprawling stems and form vine-like mats in pastures, on embankments and near old foundations. This naturalized European import is used to control erosion. A favorite flower of bumblebees and honeybees.

FLOWER: 1" cluster   **HEIGHT:** 1'–2'   **BLOOMS:** June–Aug.

Red Clover

Trifolium pratense

Pea/Bean family. Rose-purple flowers in dense rounded clusters occur on tall erect hairy stems. Alternate compound leaves are composed of three oval to oblong leaflets creased into a V-shape down the middle. Some leaves have four leaflets, the famous "Lucky Shamrock." This legume is a livestock favorite that has become naturalized after being introduced from Europe as a feed crop. Now widely found in meadows, fields and lawns.

Flower: 1"–2" clusters **Blooms:** May–Sept.
Height: 6"–24"

Phlox Moss

Phlox subulata

Phlox family. Flower has five pink to white petals with indented tips around a dark center. Narrow needle-like opposite leaves appear on creeping stems below the flowers. This naturalized garden flower "escapee" forms a moss-like carpet of colorful blooms in abandoned fields, near foundations and around cemeteries.

Flower: 3/4"   **Height:** 5"–7"   **Blooms:** April–June

223

Sweet William   *Dianthus barbatus*

PINK FAMILY. This naturalized European ornamental plant is highly variable in appearance, ranging from pink to purple to deep red. Common traits are overlapping petals in tight terminal clusters with spiked bracts and smooth lance-shaped opposite leaves. This escaped garden flower is now occasionally seen in fields and meadows.

FLOWER: ½"   **HEIGHT:** 1"–2"   **BLOOMS:** May–Sept.

Maiden Pink   *Dianthus deltoides*

PINK FAMILY. This plant has showy, pink, five-petalled
flowers with toothed edges and tiny white dots near
each flower's center. Leaf-like bracts appear under the
petals. Flower sits atop a stiff erect stem above long
narrow opposite leaves. This European garden flower
escaped cultivation and is now widespread on grassy
embankments, in fields and in meadows. Related to
the carnation, its genus name means "God's flower."

FLOWER: ½"   **HEIGHT:** 6"–12"   **BLOOMS:** June–Aug.

Soapwort

Saponaria officinalis

PINK FAMILY. Pale pink to lavender flowers in clusters appear atop stiff smooth stalks over lance- to oval-shaped leaves. Flowers have five petals with scalloped edges and indented tips. Prominent stamens emerge from the mouth of a tubular calyx. This naturalized European flower is found in open fields and pastures. Its sap contains glucoside saponin, a sudsing agent that was used by early English settlers as a soap substitute.

FLOWER: 1"   **HEIGHT:** 1'–3'   **BLOOMS:** July–Sept.

Pitcher Plant   *Sarracenia purpurea*

PITCHER PLANT FAMILY. A single nodding flower sits atop a leafless stalk with five broad purple sepals and five smaller red petals (petals fall off soon after blooming). Brownish-yellow, pitcher-shaped leaves appear in a basal rosette. Downward pointed hairs on the leaves force insects into a pool of liquid where they are dissolved by enzymes and absorbed as nutrients for the plant. This native carnivorous plant is found in acidic nutrient-poor peatland soils where its ability to digest insects helps it survive.

FLOWER: 2"   **HEIGHT:** 8"–24"   **BLOOMS:** May–Aug.

Corn Poppy

Papaver rhoeas

POPPY FAMILY. This striking flower features distinctive alternate overlapping pairs of bright red petals with a bright yellow pistil surrounded by many stamens. It sits atop a long, hairy, stalk with narrow lettuce-like leaves at the base. It was introduced to the White Mountains by colonial farmers but is becoming less common today because improved seed cleaning techniques have helped eliminate it from cultivated farmlands. This naturalized flower is found in pastures, meadows and open areas.

FLOWER: 2"–3"   **HEIGHT:** 10"–30"   **BLOOMS:** June–July

Spring Beauty *Claytonia caroliniana*

PURSLANE FAMILY. Flowers occur in clusters of two or more, on short stalks, each with five pink and white veined oval petals and two sepals. Its five stamens are each tipped with a prominent pink anther. Leaves, usually a single opposite pair, are broadly oblong-shaped with smooth edges. This native New Hampshire flower grows in large patches of rich open woods, moist thickets and streamside. Native Americans and colonists ate its potato-like bulb.

FLOWER: 1/2"–3/4" **HEIGHT:** 6"–12" **BLOOMS:** March–May

Sweet Crab Apple
Malus pumila

ROSE FAMILY. White to pinkish-white five-petalled flowers occur in clusters on branches, surrounded by finely toothed, oval leaves. The small greenish fruit of this naturalized Eurasian shrub is an important wildlife food source. It is found in fields, pastures and at woodland edges.

FLOWER: 2"   **HEIGHT:** to 25'   **BLOOMS:** May–June

Swamp Rose   *Rosa palustris*

ROSE FAMILY. This shrub has five-petalled pink flowers with numerous stamens growing on branched stems which provide cover for nesting birds. Pinnately compound alternate leaves are composed of seven, toothed leaflets. A round red fruit (rose hip) remains on the plant all winter providing a valuable wildlife food source. This native shrub is found near ponds, in wooded swamps and in marshes. Flower petals are edible and rose hips are a natural source of vitamin C.

FLOWER: 3"   **HEIGHT:** 1'–6'   **BLOOMS:** July–Aug.

Purple Flowering Raspberry   *Rubus odoratus*

ROSE FAMILY. Lavender-pink, fragrant, five-petaled flowers with numerous stamens and pistils grow in spreading clusters on thick, bristly, hair-covered stems. Alternate leaves with three-to five-pointed lobes grow on vine-like stems. This native rose bears a red, edible, though tasteless berry that is a food source for birds and mammals. It is found in rocky areas, open woods, shady embankments and thickets.

FLOWER: 1"–2"   HEIGHT: 3'–6'   BLOOMS: June–Sept.

Steeple Bush
Spiraea tomentosa

ROSE FAMILY. Numerous small pink flowers grow from a steeple-shaped terminal branched cluster. Flowers have five petals, five hairy sepals and many stamens. Leaves grow on an erect reddish stem and are oblong and toothed, alternating closely together. The leaves' undersides are covered with tangled hairs. This native plant, also known as "hardhack," is found in moist areas of overgrown fields, meadows and along shorelines.

FLOWER: 1/8"–1/4"   **HEIGHT:** 2'–4'   **BLOOMS:** July–Sept.

233

Fragrant Water-lily   *Nymphaea odorata*

WATER-LILY FAMILY. This native aquatic flower has numerous oblong pink-white petals, and several bright yellow stamens. Its floating leaves are flat, roundish and notched deeply at the base. The fragrant flowers of this native water lily open at dawn. Found in still waters of ponds and streams. Large roots, buried in muddy bottoms are a food source for muskrats.

FLOWER: 3"–5"   **HEIGHT:** 10"   **BLOOMS:** June–Sept.

Pipsissewa
Chimaphila umbellata

WINTERGREEN FAMILY. Terminal clusters of pink to white waxy fragrant flowers are seen on this native evergreen. Flowers have a five-lobed calyx with rounded petals and ten purple-tipped stamens. Shiny, lance-shaped, finely toothed leaves appear in whorls of four to six near the base of the stem. Pipsissewa is a term in the Cree language which means "it breaks into small pieces." The plant was used by Native Americans to treat kidney stones. It is found in shady areas of dry sandy woodlands.

FLOWER: ½"   **HEIGHT:** 5"–10"   **BLOOMS:** June–July

Common Wood Sorrel   *Oxalis montana*

WOOD SORREL FAMILY. A solitary pink and white flower, with dark pink veins on five notched petals and ten prominent stamens, grows on a long leafless stalk. Clover-like three-lobed compound leaves appear at the base of the plant. Leaves and flowers close at night. This low-growing native flower is found in cool, moist woodlands. Its edible leaves have a sour taste and can be toxic if eaten in large doses due to the presence of oxalic acid.

FLOWER: ³/₄"   **HEIGHT:** 3"–6"   **BLOOMS:** May–July

Jack-in-the-pulpit *Arisaema triphyllum*

ARUM FAMILY. A brownish-purple, striped spathe (pulpit) curls like a hooded flap over a club-shaped spadix (Jack) composed of tightly compressed small brown flowers. One to two long-stalked, divided leaves with three veined leaflets overshadow the spathe. The plant fruits a cluster of red berries that are a favorite food source of game birds and bear. Native Americans ground its turnip-like root for food. This native member of the arum family is found in rich, wet woodlands and swamps.

FLOWER: 2"–3" high **HEIGHT:** 1'–3' **BLOOMS:** April–June

Arrow Arum   *Peltandra virginica*

ARUM FAMILY. This aquatic native arum has a leaf-like spathe and an elongated spadix with female flowers at its base and male flowers at its top. Broad, arrow-shaped leaves are long-stalked with deep veins and rippled edges. Its green-brown berries are an important food source for wood ducks and marsh birds. Colonists and Native Americans ate the roots of this plant when food supplies ran low. Large colonies are found in ponds, swamps, marshes and waterways.

FLOWER: 4"–7" spadix   **BLOOMS:** May–July
HEIGHT: 1'–2'

Skunk Cabbage   *Symplocarpus foetidus*

ARUM FAMILY. A cluster of pale, tightly wrinkled flowers is almost completely enclosed by a purple-brown spathe with a curled point. Large, bright green stalked cabbage-like leaves with deep veins emerge after the flower blooms. A pungent skunk odor comes from the mature plant. This native early spring flower grows in wet woody bogs and its seeds are a food source for waterfowl and other birds. Native Americans used its crushed root to dress wounds.

FLOWER: 3"–6"   **HEIGHT:** 1'–2'   **BLOOMS:** March–May

Blue Cohosh — *Caulophyllum thalictroides*

BARBERRY FAMILY. Greenish-brown flowers with six petal-like sepals, six small curled petals, six yellow stamens and a single pistil appear in branching terminal clusters. Fruit is a dark blue poisonous berry atop a thick stalk. Plant has two compound leaves each divided into many smaller, lobed leaflets. A native of New Hampshire's rich moist woodland areas, it is known to cause contact dermatitis. Its folk name, "squaw root," is derived from its use by Native Americans to induce labor.

FLOWER: ½"   **HEIGHT:** 1'–3'   **BLOOMS:** April–June

Staghorn Sumac

Rhus hirta

CASHEW FAMILY. This native flowering shrub receives its common name from the thick downy hairs that cover its branches and stem giving the appearance of a "stag's horn." Pyramid-shaped terminal clusters of greenish-brown flowers rise above compound leaves composed of ten to twenty sharp-edged toothed leaflets. It is found in dry soils in fields, clearings and meadows. Its fruit is an important source of food for birds during the winter.

FLOWERS: 8" clusters **HEIGHT:** 3'–20' **BLOOMS:** June–July

Poison Ivy   *Toxicodendron rydbergii*

SUMAC FAMILY. Simple branching clusters of small greenish flowers grow from the leaf axils of this notorious creeping rhizomatous vine. Stems are woody and show leaf scars. Leaves have three lobes and are smooth-edged with a few teeth. Emerging leaves are shiny and reddish. All parts of the poison ivy plant cause severe allergic reactions especially if inhaled while burning. This native plant is found along stonewalls, in thickets and open woodlands.

FLOWER: 1/8"   **HEIGHT:** 1'–4'   **BLOOMS:** May–Aug.

Common Cat-tail   *Typha latifolia*

CAT-TAIL FAMILY. Cylinder-like terminal clusters of minuscule flowers appear atop a long thick stem. Yellow stamenate (male) flowers grow above brown pistillate (female) flowers. The male flowers bloom before the female flowers, insuring cross-pollination. Leaves are long, narrow and reed-like. This New Hampshire native plant forms dense stands in the shallow waters of wetland marshes and swamps. Native Americans cooked the starchy young flower spikes like corn.

FLOWER: 6" spikes   HEIGHT: 3'–9'   BLOOMS: May–June

Early Fly Honeysuckle   *Lonicera canadensis*

HONEYSUCKLE FAMILY. Twin funnel-shaped flowers droop from the branches of this shrub. Flowers are greenish-yellow with five equal short lobes and mature into red berries. Leaves are oval, stalked, and appear opposite on branches. This native woodland shrub attracts bees and flies for its pollination.

FLOWER: ³/₄"   HEIGHT: 2'–5'   BLOOMS: April–May

Arrowwood
Viburnum dentatum

HONEYSUCKLE FAMILY. The flat-topped clusters of this native shrub bloom into many small five-petalled greenish-white flowers. Oval to heart-shaped shiny leaves have coarse, sharp-toothed edges, and appear beneath flower clusters on woody stems. Fruits occur in clusters of purple-black berries. This shrub is found in wet wooded areas, near swamps and near ponds.

FLOWER: ¹/₄"   **HEIGHT:** 3'–15'   **BLOOMS:** May–Aug.

Indian Cucumber Root   *Medeola virginiana*

LILY FAMILY. One or more small nodding yellow flowers lie hidden beneath the upper leaves. Flowers have three recurved petals and three recurved petal-like sepals. Leaves are found in two whorls around an erect central stem. The upper whorl is composed of three small lance-shaped leaves. The lower whorl appears at mid stem and is composed of six to ten larger lance-shaped leaves. Native Americans ate the cucumber-like root but this practice is discouraged today because the plant is not common. It is found in enriched moist woods.

FLOWER: ½"   **HEIGHT:** 1'–3'   **BLOOMS:** May–June

Smooth Solomon's Seal

Polygonatum biflorum

LILY FAMILY. Two to ten pairs of greenish bell-shaped flowers hang beneath a smooth arching stem. Flowers hang below large, smooth, oval leaves with prominent parallel veins. In late summer flowers are replaced by berries which are an important food source for game birds. This native New Hampshire herb is found in dry to moist woods and thickets.

FLOWER: 1/2"–3/4"   **HEIGHT:** 1'–3'   **BLOOMS:** May–June

Hairy Solomon's Seal *Polygonatum pubescens*

LILY FAMILY. Two to eight small, greenish-white bell-like flowers hang on arching stems amid shiny parallel-veined broadly lance-shaped hairy leaves. Native Americans and European settlers ate the starchy potato-like rhizome. This native perennial gets its common name from the Solomon's seal stamp-shaped scars left where the leaf stalk is separated from the rhizome. The berries of this flower are known to cause vomiting if eaten. Found in dry to moist woodlands.

FLOWER: ½" HEIGHT: 8"–36" BLOOMS: May–June

False Hellebore   *Veratrum viride*

LILY FAMILY. In the spring this plant's large oval green leaves with their prominent parallel veins are seen in small to large stands in wetlands throughout the region. As the leaves wilt, a tall branching stem is covered with small star-shaped hairy greenish flowers. The bitter roots and leaves of this plant are potentially fatal if eaten. Legend says that some Native American tribes used False Hellebore to test the strength of their leaders. Those who consumed the largest quantities of the plant, and survived, were fit to lead the tribe.

FLOWER: ½"   **HEIGHT:** 2'–7'   **BLOOMS:** May–July

Spotted Coral Root   *Corallorhiza maculata*

ORCHID FAMILY. Ten or more small flowers alternate up a leafless stem. Flowers have three petals, two curved lateral petals tinged with purple, and a spotted lip petal hanging below. The three sepals are curved and spreading. This native orchid has no leaves for photosynthesis so it depends on fungus in the soil to supply nutrients. It is found in moist, sandy to loamy forests.

FLOWER: 1"   **HEIGHT:** 9"–30"   **BLOOMS:** June–Aug.

Rattlesnake Plantain   *Goodyera pubescens*

ORCHID FAMILY. Very small greenish white flowers bloom along the upper quarter of a stout vertical stem. The flower's upper sepal and two upper petals form a hood. Lateral sepals are egg-shaped and the lip petal is short and downwardly curved. Rosettes of three or more oblong basal leaves form near the ground. The leaves are ornately veined in white, and thus said to resemble rattlesnake's scales. This native orchid forms colonies through a creeping rhizome. It is found in dry to damp woodland areas.

FLOWER: ¼"   **HEIGHT:** 6"–20"   **BLOOMS:** July–Sept.

Club Spur Orchis   *Platanthera clavellata*

ORCHID FAMILY. Ten to fifty small green flowers are arranged around a vertical stem over a single, long, lance-shaped leaf at the base of the stem. The lower lip is toothed and has a blunt tip as if the lip was cut off. The spur has a club-like thickening at its end. This native orchid is found in wet woodlands, damp meadows, seeps and bogs.

FLOWER: ¹/₄"   HEIGHT: 6"–18"   BLOOMS: July–Aug.

Northern Green Orchid
Platanthera hyperborea

ORCHID FAMILY. The flowers of this small native orchid are said to resemble the hooded parkas of arctic explorers. It is named after the Hyberboreans, a mythical tribe who lived in constant sunlight above the Arctic Circle. Its small green flowers spiral up a vertical stem intertwined with lance-shaped leaves. The upper sepal and two upper petals form a hood. The lower lip petal is forward-curved and the spur is short and club-shaped. Found in open to shady, moist to dry woodland areas.

FLOWER: $1/3$"–$1/2$"   HEIGHT: 1'–2'   BLOOMS: June–Aug.

Ragged Fringed Orchid   *Platanthera lacera*

ORCHID FAMILY. Small greenish-white flowers surround the upper third of a vertical stem. This orchid has three sepals and three petals with the upper sepal and two upper petals forming a forward-curved hood. The lateral sepals are egg-shaped and spread out to the sides. The lower "lip petal" is deeply lobed into three heavily fringed sections, hence the species name *lacera* (Latin for lacerated). Two or more lance-shaped leaves appear near the base. This native orchid is found in many environments from high elevations to deep lowland woods.

FLOWER: ³/₄"–1"   **HEIGHT:** 12"–30"   **BLOOMS:** July–Aug.

Round-leaved Orchid   *Platanthera orbiculata*

ORCHID FAMILY. Ten to thirty small green orchid flowers are loosely clustered atop a slender leafless stalk. Two large, round, veined basal leaves lie flat on the ground. Flowers have a fringeless lower lip and a rear-facing pointed spur up to one inch long. This, and the almost identical *Platanthera macrophylla,* (the *P. macrophylla* has a spur generally longer than an inch), are found in mixed hardwood forests at elevations up to the alpine zone.

FLOWER: 1"   **HEIGHT:** 1'–2'   **BLOOMS:** June–Aug.

Ground Nut   *Apios americana*

Pea/Bean family. Reddish-brown, helmet-shaped flowers appear in tightly packed clusters on short stalks which grow from the leaf axils of this climbing vine. Pinnately compound leaves are composed of three to seven oval to lance-shaped leaflets. Native Americans ate the potato-like tubers of this native vine. This wild food source is credited with saving early English settlers from starvation. Later, Native Americans were prohibited by English law from harvesting this important food crop on lands claimed by England.

Flower: 2"–4"   **Height:** 10' vine   **Blooms:** July–Sept.

Illustrated Glossary

FLOWER STRUCTURES

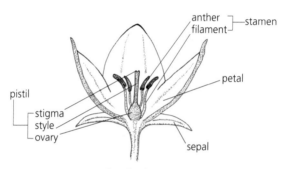

anther
filament ⎱ stamen

petal

pistil
⎧ stigma
⎨ style
⎩ ovary

sepal

Simple Flower

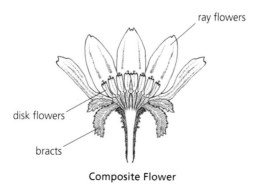

ray flowers

disk flowers

bracts

Composite Flower

FLOWER SHAPES

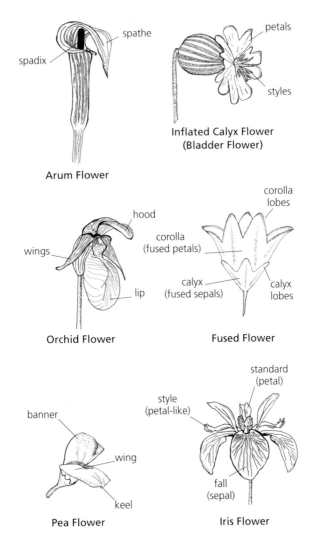

spathe

spadix

Arum Flower

petals

styles

**Inflated Calyx Flower
(Bladder Flower)**

hood

wings

lip

Orchid Flower

corolla
lobes

corolla
(fused petals)

calyx
(fused sepals)

calyx
lobes

Fused Flower

banner

wing

keel

Pea Flower

standard
(petal)

style
(petal-like)

fall
(sepal)

Iris Flower

SIMPLE LEAF SHAPES

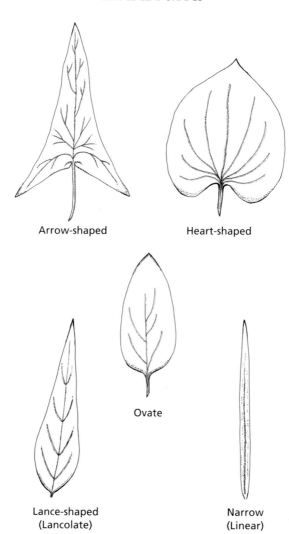

Arrow-shaped

Heart-shaped

Ovate

Lance-shaped
(Lancolate)

Narrow
(Linear)

COMPOUND LEAF PARTS

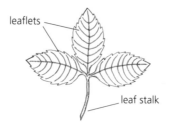

leaflets

leaf stalk

COMPOUND LEAF SHAPES

Pinnately Divided

Palm-like
(Palmately Divided)

LEAF MARGINS (EDGES)

Dissected

Entire
(Smooth-edged)

Lobed

Toothed

LEAF ARRANGEMENTS

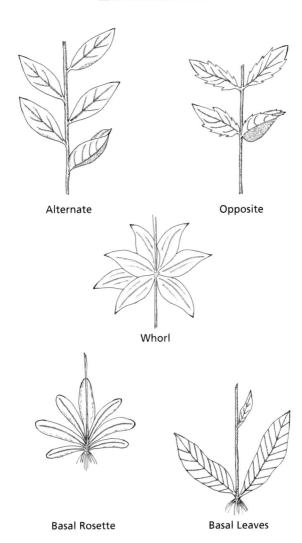

Alternate

Opposite

Whorl

Basal Rosette

Basal Leaves

LEAF ATTACHMENTS

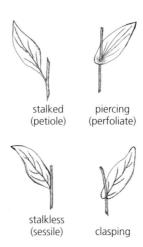

stalked
(petiole)

piercing
(perfoliate)

stalkless
(sessile)

clasping

STEM AND STALK ARRANGEMENTS

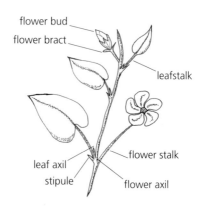

flower bud

flower bract

leafstalk

flower stalk

leaf axil

stipule

flower axil

Glossary

Alpine Zone. The area above the tree line. In the White Mountains this region is found near the summits of the higher peaks.

Alternate. Refers to an arrangement of leaves or flowers, appearing first on one side, then farther up on the other side of a stem or stalk, alternating back and forth.

Annual. A plant whose life cycle is complete in one year.

Anther. The pollen-bearing tip of the stamen.

Axil. The upper angle formed between a leaf stalk and a stem.

Basal. At or near the base of a plant or stem.

Beard. Small tufts of hairs usually appearing on the inner surface of a petal.

Biennial. A plant whose life cycle takes two years; leaves appearing the first year, the flower usually appearing in the second year.

Bract. A small leaf, usually not fully developed, associated with a flower, usually appearing near the base of the flower.

Calyx. A term describing all the sepals of a flower taken together.

Calyx flower. A flower whose sepals are fused into one structure, sometimes with lobes at its tip.

Chlorophyll. A green-tinted chemical which plants create and use to capture the energy of sunlight and store that energy as food.

Clasping leaf. A stalkless leaf that encircles its stem either wholly (*clasping*) or part way (*partly clasping*).

Composite flower. A flower composed of many smaller flowers appearing together in a unified flower head that appears from a distance to be a single simple flower.

Compound leaf. A leaf composed of several distinct leaflets.

Contact dermatitis. An allergic reaction which occurs when some plants are touched.

Corolla. A term describing all the petals of a flower taken together.

Corolla flower. A flower whose petals are fused into one structure, frequently with petal shaped lobes at its tip.

Corymb. A flat-topped flower cluster with outer flowers being on longer stems or branches so that all the flowers appear at approximately the same height.

Disk flower. A small tube-shaped flower which appears in the central disk of composite flowers in the Aster family. In most cases disk flowers are surrounded by ray flowers.

Entire. Refers to the smooth edge of a leaf, that is an edge without teeth, lobes, waves, etc.

Escapee. Refers to a flower which has escaped from cultivation in a garden or farm.

Filament. The stalk-shaped structure which supports the anther.

Floret. A small flower, usually incomplete, that is often part of a larger flower head.

Flower. The reproductive organ of a plant having stamens, pistils or both, usually surrounded first by an inner ring of petals, and second, by an outer ring of sepals.

Flower head. The whole "bouquet" of tiny flowers that appear together in a composite flower and which appear to be a single flower from a distance. Also used informally to refer to all of a flower's parts taken as a whole: petals, sepals, pistils, stamens, etc.

Glabrous. Hairless.

Herb. A plant that does not have a woody stem. Also used informally to indicate plants cultivated for use as flavorings or as medicinals.

Herbaceous. The quality of having a non-woody stem and stalks.

Lanceolate. Lance-shaped. Widest below the middle, usually much longer than wide, with a pointed tip and pointed or rounded at the base. (See leaf diagram.)

Leaflet. The individual leafy parts of a compound leaf. Often leaflets appear to be whole leaves at first glance.

Legume. A plant belonging to the Pea/Bean family.

Mesic. Rich in soil moisture.

Native. Refers to a flower that is found in an area without having been introduced there by human activity.

Naturalized. Refers to a plant that is introduced to an area by human activity and that sustains itself in the wild without further care. (Whether a flower is naturalized is sometimes questionable because periodic human intervention can sometimes perpetuate a species which might otherwise die out. Escaped garden flowers which live for years at the edges of mowed fields and pastures are an example of questionable naturalization.)

Nodding. Bent over, hanging down.

Oblong. A long oval shape often with flattened sides, usually more than twice as long as wide.

Opposite. Leaves that appear directly across from each other on the stem.

Oval. Broadly elliptical in shape, nearly half as wide as long.

Ovary. The base of the pistil which contains the unfertilized seeds.

Palmate. Refers to an arrangement of leaves growing from a single point in a shape similar to the branches of a palm tree. Can also refer to a lobed or divided leaf whose parts all meet at a single point.

Palmately compound. An arrangement of leaflets in a palm shape.

Parasitic. Refers to a plant that lives off the food of another plant rather than making its food through photosynthesis. Some plants are *semi-parasitic*, making some of their food through photosynthesis and deriving some of their food from other plants.

Pedicel. The stalk of a flower.

Perennial. A plant which lives for many years, blooming at regular intervals.

Petals. A series of leaf-like structures, usually colorful, that surround the stamen and pistil of a flower; used to attract pollinating insects.

Photosynthesis. The process whereby plants use chlorophyll to convert the energy of sunlight into food.

Pinnate. A leaf arrangement where the leaflets are arranged opposite or alternately along a stalk (see compound leaf shapes diagram).

Pistil. The seed bearing organ of the flower often referred to as the "female" reproductive organ, consisting of the *ovary* which holds the immature seeds, the *style* a tubular structure which forms the entrance to the ovary, and the *stigma*, the tip of the pistil that receives pollen.

Pollen. In wildflowers, pollen forms in the anthers. When pollen is transferred to the stigma, the pollen divides into male cells which then move down the style toward the flower's ovary. Those cells then fertilize the immature seeds, thus initiating sexual reproduction.

Pubescent. Having a covering of fine hairs.

Ray flowers. Petal-shaped flowers that appear in a ring around disk flowers. Usually each ray flower has a small stamen on its upper side.

Rhizome. An underground stem that runs horizontally under the ground, usually sending up new flowering stems.

Sepals. Leaves that usually appear in a ring outside the petals. Sepals may resemble the flower's petals.

Shrub. A flowering plant with a woody stem.

Sinus. An empty space outlined by a leaf's lobes or a leaf's curled edges.

Spadix. A tightly-formed, spike-shaped flower cluster in the center of flower heads in the Arum family.

Spathe. A leafy structure that surrounds and protects the spadix in flowers of the Arum family.

Stalk. The supporting structure of a flower or a leaf.

Stamens. The male reproductive organ of a flower consisting of the anther (which holds the pollen) supported by the filament.

Stem. The main supporting structure of the plant.

Stemless. A term used in categorizing violets. Stemless violets do not have a central stem, rather the flowers and leaves grow on their own separate stalks.

Stemmed. A term used in categorizing violets. Stemmed violets have a central stem from which leaf stalks and flower stalks branch off.

Stigma. The tip of the pistil that receives pollen.

Stipule. A small leaf-like appendage found at the base of a leaf stalk.

Style. The mid-portion of the female reproductive organ of a flower, the part of the pistil between the ovary and the stigma.

Talus slope. Fallen rocks and rubble which collect beneath cliffs.

Umbel. An umbrella-shaped cluster of flowers.

Upland. An area of landscape with moist to well-drained soils: forests, wetlands, fields, etc.

Wetland. An area of landscape that is saturated or inundated with water during the growing season.

Whorl(s). A circular arrangement of flowers, petals, or leaves, usually around a stem or stalk. (See leaf diagram.)

Further Reading

We consulted many fine botanical manuals and wildflower guides in the preparation of this book. Listed below are some that we recommend for further reading and exploration.

Angier, Bradford. *Field Guide to Medicinal Wild Plants.* Harrisburg, PA: Stackpole Books, 1978. This beautifully hand-illustrated reference has interesting discussions of the medicinal uses of many wildflowers encountered in the White Mountains.

Capon, Brian. *Botany for Gardeners: An Introduction and Guide.* Portland, Oregon: Timber Press, 1990. A well-illustrated introduction to the basic principles of botany. Flower structures and their role in plant reproduction are clearly illustrated and explained for the amateur botanist.

Chapman, William K. *Orchids of the Northeast: A Field Guide.* Syracuse, NY: Syracuse University Press, 1997.

A complete guide to this family of wildflowers. Illustrated with photos and in-depth plant and habitat descriptions.

Cox, Donald D. *Common Flowering Plants of the Northeast: Their Natural History and Uses.* Albany, NY: State University of New York Press, 1985. A concise one volume reference to Northeastern flowers. It is illustrated with accurate pen and ink drawings and has a helpful key. Unlike many other one volume guides the main divisions of the book are organized, not by color, but rather by setting: woodlands, fields, wetlands, salty soils. Very helpful for identification if you know the setting of the plant.

Gleason, Henry, and Arthur Cronquist. *Manual of Vascular Plants of the Northeastern United States and Adjacent Canada.* Bronx, NY: New York Botanical Garden, 1991. A very complete botanical reference with a thorough identification key. It has an accompanying volume with exquisite illustrations clearly depicting the important structures which distinguish similar species.

Magee, Dennis W. and Harry E. Ahles. *Flora of the Northeast: A Manual of the Vascular Flora of New England and Adjacent New York*. Amherst, MA: University of Massachusetts Press, 1999. Currently one of the primary desk references for keying and identifying flowers in the Northeast. It has helpful county by county maps indicating sightings of a given species. In depth keys and illustrations help distinguish species and variations. Covers thousands of species in hundreds of families.

Newcomb, Lawrence. *Newcomb's Wildflower Guide.* Boston, MA: Little, Brown and Company, 1997. Now a classic, this guide has a quick and effective key system based upon answering five basic questions about a plant's structure. Handsomely illustrated with black and white and color drawings.

Peterson, Roger Tory and Margaret McKenny. *A Field Guide to Wildflowers of Northeastern and North-central North America.* Boston, MA: Houghton Mifflin Company, 1968. This classic guide has helpful descriptions and quality black and white and color illustrations of hundreds of flowers in this area.

Slack, Nancy G. and Allison W. Bell. *Appalachian Mountain Club Field Guide to the New England Alpine Summits.* Boston, MA: Appalachian Mountain Club Books, 1995. This concise, photographically illustrated introduction to the alpine summits gives a great overview of the geology, ecology and the plant and animal inhabitants of the alpine areas of the White Mountains.

Sperduto, Daniel D. *A Classification of Wetland Natural Comunities in New Hampshire.* New Hampshire Natural Heritage Inventory, Department of Resources and Economic Development, Concord, NH, 2000a.

Sperduto, Daniel D. *A Guide to the Natural Comunities in New Hampshire.* Interim version. New Hampshire Natural Heritage Inventory, Department of Resources and Economic Development, Concord, NH, 2000b.

Taylor, James, Thomas D. Lee and Laura F. McCarthy (eds.) *New Hampshire's Living Legacy: The Biodiversity of the Granite State.* Concord, NH: New Hampshire Fish and Game Department, 1996. An interesting and concise introduction to contemporary views on natural communities, including the wildflowers found in those communities and the importance of stewardship and conservation of wilderness resources.

Thieret, John W. (revising author), William A Niering and Nancy C. Olmstead. *National Audubon Society Field Guide to North American Wildflowers Eastern Region, Revised Edition.* New York, NY: Alfred A. Knopf, 2001. An in-depth guide with useful descriptions of most species in the eastern United States.

Thompson, Elizabeth H. and Eric R. Sorenson. *Wetland, Woodland, Wildland: A Guide to the Natural Communities of Vermont.* Hanover, NH: University Press of New England, 2000. Although oriented toward the natural communities found in Vermont, it has excellent descriptions of most of the natural communities found in the White Mountain area, including descriptions of the ecology, physical setting, primary vegetation and characteristic plants.

Species at Risk

S everal of the plants in this book are rare. The New Hampshire Natural Heritage Bureau (NHNHB) is the state program in the Division of Forests and Lands that finds, tracks, and facilitates the protection of New Hampshire's rare plants and exemplary natural communities.

Rare plants are categorized by New Hampshire Natural Heritage as:

Endangered. Five or less documented occurrences or critically imperiled.

Threatened. Six to 20 documented occurrences, or imperiled due to rarity.

On Watch. Twenty-one to 100 documented occurrences or which may, in the opinion of plant experts, become threatened.

New Hampshire Natural Heritage encourages anyone who believes they have observed a rare plant to contact the NHNHB office and report their observations.

When observing rare plants it is important to remember not to damage the plants or their habitat. Alpine wildflowers, for example, are threatened primarily by people who walk off established trails and trample the fragile plants and soils. In addition, endangered and threatened species are protected under the New Hampshire Native Plant Protection Act, which prohibits picking or disturbing those plants unless you are the owner of the land on which they grow.

Training in finding and reporting rare wildflowers is available from the New England Wildflower Society's Plant Conservation Volunteer program mentioned in the *Wildflower Resources*.

Forms for reporting rare plants can be obtained from the New Hampshire Natural Heritage Bureau office in Concord, New Hampshire (603) 271-3623 or from the website at www.nhdfl. org.

Wildflower Resources

The following organizations help preserve and maintain the wilderness lands and nature preserves in which many of the wildflowers in our book were photographed. These organizations offer membership, educational programs, trail access and volunteer opportunities for wildflower enthusiasts of all ages.

The Appalachian Mountain Club (AMC) is a nonprofit membership and volunteer organization which protects the mountains, rivers and trails of the Appalachian regions. Through trail maintenance, hut systems and educational programs, the AMC provides outdoor recreational opportunities for all ages. Wildflower viewing is abundant on the AMC trail system and during the summer months resident naturalists at the AMC huts and base lodges conduct daily educational programs, many of which cover wildflowers seen in the White Mountains. For membership information and educational program calendars contact the

AMC Pinkham Notch Visitor Center, Route 16, Pinkham Notch, NH (603) 466-2727, or go to their website at www. outdoors.org.

The Audubon Society of New Hampshire is a membership organization whose mission is to protect and enhance New Hampshire's natural environment for wildlife and people. It maintains over 10,000 acres of wildlife habitats throughout the state of New Hampshire. It operates seven nature centers, which feature educational exhibits and programs. In addition, ASNH maintains twenty-seven wildlife sanctuaries where visitors of all ages have access to nature trails, many of which feature outstanding examples of native wildflowers. For visitor information and volunteer opportunities, contact ASNH, 3 Silk Farm Rd., Concord, NH 03301. Call (603) 224-9909 or go to their website at www.nhaudubon.org.

The **Nature Conservancy** is a leading wilderness conservation organization. The New Hampshire chapter, with its conservation partners, has protected more than 119,000 acres of critical natural lands in New Hampshire, including 26 nature preserves. For more than 50 years the Conservancy's mission has been to preserve the plants, animals and natural communities that represent the diversity of life on earth by protecting the lands and waters they need to survive. For information on volunteer and land protection opportunities, visit their website at www.nature.org/newhampshire or call (603) 224-5853.

The New England Wild Flower Society is the nation's oldest institution dedicated to the conservation of wild plants. The Society's mission is "to promote the conservation of temperate north American flora through education, research, horticulture, habitat preservation, and advocacy". The Society teaches thousands of people every year about native plants and their habitats through courses, field trips, garden tours, teacher training and publications, including its membership magazine "New England Wild Flower." The Society owns and operates Garden in the Woods, in Framingham, Massachusetts, the largest landscaped collection of wildflowers in the northeast. The 45-acre garden is open to the public from mid-April through October.

In addition, the Society owns and maintains the *Plainfield Sanctuary* in Plainfield, NH. This sanctuary features an unusually diverse assemblage of wildflower and fern species which can viewed from the road which winds through its 86 wooded acres. Plants include lime-loving species, woodland wildflowers and riverbank flora.

In addition, the Society operates the *New England Plant Conservation Program (NEPCoP)* which is a collaboration among botanists, federal and state agencies, and conservation organizations which trains volunteers to report and document sightings of wildflowers. Phone 508-877-7630 or go to their website at www.newfs.org for more information on membership and volunteer opportunities and for directions to sanctuaries and gardens.

The Society for the Protection of New Hampshire Forest (SPNHF) is the largest and oldest non-profit land conservation group in New Hampshire. It manages over 100 forest sites located throughout the state, many with self guided nature trails. Many interesting wild-flowers can be seen in these varied eco-systems.

The society maintains a visitor center, a nature garden and hiking trails at its Concord headquarters free of charge. For more information and a map of SPNHF sites in New Hampshire contact SPNHF, 54 Portsmouth Street, Concord, NH 03301. Call (603) 224-9945 or go to their website at www.spnhf.org.

Weeks State Park on the slopes of Mt. Prospect in Lancaster, New Hampshire has a series of nature trails with abundant wildflower viewing. The top of Mt. Prospect offers stunning views of the Presidential Mountains and has a fire tower open to the public. A variety of educational programs (including flower and nature walks and a northeast hawk watch) is offered by the Weeks State Park Association, a nonprofit membership organization. For information on programs and activities call (603) 788-4004.

Quincy Bog Natural Area is a 44-acre wildlife preserve with a one-mile self-guided ecological trail which follows the bog shoreline, adjacent woodland and wetland areas and finally crosses a beaver dam. This well marked and well maintained trail is suitable for family and school outings as well as providing interesting sightings for the experienced naturalist. This preserve has a nature center and a resident ecologist during summer. It is located on Quincy Road in Rumney, New Hampshire. Quincy Bog is maintained by volunteers and private donations. For directions and a guide to the trail, write to Quincy Bog Natural Area, P.O. Box

90, Rumney, NH 03266 or go to their website at www. quincybog.org.

The Squam Lakes Natural Science Center is located at the southern edge of the White Mountains. This family oriented science center offers a well rounded introduction to the animal and plant life of the White Mountains. The main trail features exhibits of local animals in their natural settings. In addition, there are several other self guided trails that traverse many different ecosystems. Many of the flowers depicted in this book can be seen while walking these well maintained trails. These manageable trails are a great alternative to more remote hikes and provide a method of introducing children to the diversity of New Hampshire's wildlife.

The science center is also home to *Kirkwood Gardens,* where many varieties of native and non-native wildflowers are displayed in a formal garden setting. Entrance to Kirkwood Gardens is free but there is a fee to enter the nature exhibits at the science center. Call (603) 968-7194 or visit www.nhnature.org for information on membership, programs and directions.

United States Forest Service. The Forest Service maintains ranger stations and public information centers throughout the White Mountain National Forest where information on trails, wildlife, camping sites, hiking and parking are provided.

Please note that within the White Mountain National Forest the Code of Federal Regulations protects wildflowers, which are considered public property, and picking wildflowers on public lands is prohibited. In addition, many areas of the White Mountain National Forest require a parking pass. Passes can be obtained for a fee at forest service information centers and at drop boxes at many locations. For more information please contact the information centers and ranger stations listed below.

Pemigewasset Ranger Station
Route 175
Plymouth, NH 03264
(603) 536-1315

Saco Ranger Station
RFD#1, Box 94
Conway, NH 03818
(603) 447-5448

Androscoggin Ranger Station
300 Glen Road
Gorham, NH 03581
(603) 466-2713

Ammonoosuc Ranger Station
660 Trudeau Road
Bethlehem, NH 03574
(603) 869-2626

Lincoln Woods Information Center
Kancamagus Highway
(Rte. 112, 4 miles east of exit 32, I-93)

Evans Notch Information Center
18 Mayville Rd.
Bethel, ME 04217
(207) 824-2134

Index